MW00638883

SOARING
BETWEEN
PASTORS

8 Actions to Thrive During a Pastoral Transition

TOM HARRIS
WITH GEORGE BULLARD

BIG SNOWY
Media

Library of Congress Cataloging-in-Publication Data
Soaring Between Pastors: 8 Actions to Thrive During a Pastoral Transition
(Big Snowy Media)
Includes index.
1. Religion 2. Spirituality
I. Title
ISBN 978-0-578-91074-1

To My Sister

My sister, Linda Jean Harris (1949-2020), was one of the greatest loves of my life. Her "sweetheart" and "I love you" still sing in my ear.

Linda had a hard life. She was born with an intellectual disability, a hole in her heart, and psoriasis. At age 18, she developed paranoid schizophrenia and experienced periodic breaks with reality, hallucinations, and mental hospital stays. Linda spent the last fifteen years at a nursing home with her beloved cat, Dewdrop. Linda loved and constantly solicited new teddy bears, and her soft-hearted brother came through, giving her over 500 of those furry friends.

As Linda aged, her life became more difficult with the added complications of heart disease, runaway diabetes, arthritis, and finally, lungs full of blood clots. In early 2020, the nursing home called and said that Linda was unresponsive. The following day I flew to her, and to the surprise of the nurses and staff, she opened her eyes and rallied. For the next seven days, I stood by Linda's bed as we talked, held hands, and I attended to her every need until the second the Lord called her home.

I began this writing project six months before Linda's death. When I told Linda I was writing a book, she was both surprised and amazed. She said, "I want one" I replied, "Linda, you will get a hand-signed copy."

I dedicate this book to Linda. It is my signature of love.

Contents

Acknowledgement

T hank you, George Bullard, for partnering with me in the writing of this book. You are one of America's foremost authorities in church health, vision, and organizational development. I have the utmost respect for you, your walk with the Lord, and your knowledge. It's an honor to have you as co-author.

The Interim Pastor Ministries Board of Directors authorized and funded through our general fund, the writing and publishing of this book. Thank you, Noah Palmer, Ken Moberg, Rick Thompson, Terry Shanahan, Jon Payne, Mike Shields, and Steve Welling. Your friendship and partnership have enriched my life and ministry.

Norman Jameson, you did the initial copy editing, and I thank you. You helped when writer's block and fatigue loomed. Your fingerprints are on this book. Thank you. It is a joy to call you a friend!

Seven IPM interim pastors wrote the case studies from their personal interim pastor experience. Gordon Simms, Rick Foster, Will Hope, Dan Wertman, Jim Fleming, John Strubhar, Mike Moran—you are top-tier Seasoned, Skilled and Strategic Intentional Interim Pastors. You make churches soar! Thank you for your stories that illustrated the concepts in each chapter.

Finally, I thank our Triune God for the call of salvation and service. "Jesus paid it all and all to Him, I owe." Thank you for making my later years of ministry my most fruitful and rewarding season of gospel service. You have stretched me to no end and taken me further and higher than I ever imagined. All to Your glory! Hallelujah and Amen!

Tom Harris

Introduction

I f your church does not currently have a pastor, you are getting ready to read the most important book in your church's life. No other book on leadership, church growth, spiritual formation, missional engagement, church administration, stewardship and generosity, security and safety, or numerous other practical topics will help your congregation thrive during a pastoral transition like this book.

Read this book before you take any significant actions during a pastoral transition. If you take the eight actions described in this book, your church will soar between pastors. Talk about this book with your key leadership. Begin gathering your congregation now to pray and seek God's leadership and guidance during this pastoral transition. Your goal should be to secure a P³ Lead Pastor who is *passionate*, *proactive*, and *personable*.

A P³ Lead Pastor is *passionate* about the Good News of Jesus Christ and is gifted in preaching and teaching this Good News. *Proactivity* characterizes a P³ Lead Pastor, especially in the areas of vision casting and fulfillment, and developing disciples prepared to serve as leaders in the church. A P³ Lead Pastor is *personable*. They love to be with people, encouraging them in discipleship and nurturing them through the stages of life, with all its predictable and unpredictable events. In Action Seven, you will find a detailed explanation of a P³ Lead Pastor.

Using an S³ Intentional Interim Pastor who is *seasoned, skilled,* and *strategic* is a great way to help you transition to a P³ Lead Pastor. An S³ Intentional Interim Pastor is not a newbie. They are seasoned in leading churches between pastors to reach their full Kingdom potential. Because they are seasoned, they will seldom encounter a church situation they have not already experienced. These Intentional Interim Pastors have above average ministerial *skills* and will be able to lead the church with grace and style during the transition between pastors. *Strategic* actions that enable the church to make progress between pastors come naturally to them. In Action Eight, you will find a detailed description of an S³ Intentional Interim Pastor.

As you prepare for your next lead pastor, your Intentional Interim Pastor can help your church discern and craft its ministry as a C³ Soaring Church characterized by D³ Intentionality. A C³ Soaring Church's missional directive is the *Great Commission* in the spirit of the *Great Commandment*. It has deep ownership of its *enduring core values* and is *captured by a vision* that comes not from the next pastor or the leaders but from God himself. Action Five explains in greater detail the identity and work of a C³ church.

A C³ Church lives out God's mission in a manner that affirms its core values, using D³ Intentionality to fulfill God's captivating, empowering vision. A D³ church focuses on (1) *disciple-making* processes and programs, (2) *developing leaders,* (3) *dynamic strategies* and *tactics* that are agile, innovative, and continually transitioning and changing. Chapter six

---

SOARING BETWEEN PASTORS FRAMEWORK

S3 Intentional Interim Pastor

Seasoned, **S**killed, **S**trategic

+

C³ Soaring Church

Great **C**ommission, Enduring **C**ore Values, **C**aptured by Vision

+

D³ Intentionality

Disciple-making, **D**eveloping Leaders, **D**ynamic Innovation

=

P³ Lead Pastor

Passionate, **P**roactive, **P**ersonable

---

addresses D^3 Intentionality.

The formula implied here is that $S^3 + C^3 + D^3 = P^3$. An S^3 Intentional Interim Pastor can help develop a C^3 Soaring Church with D^3 Intentionality to potentially lead to a P^3 Lead Pastor who can help the church to soar continually. The new lead pastor will regularly clarify the C^3 and D^3 characteristics and deepen their impact.

This book details the eight actions you can take in the interim between pastors so your church can soar and thrive—not just survive. To help you soar, we recommend the services of an S^3 Intentional Interim Pastor.

Far from being a dead period, a pastoral transition can help your church come alive with missional promise. Do not view the transition as a period to get through as quickly as possible. Consider it an open door of opportunity for your church to soar between pastors in the direction of God's full Kingdom potential.

The transition between pastors, whatever the cause, is an opportune time to regroup, self-examine, take specific actions, address barriers, deepen spirituality, strengthen leadership and programs, and discern a shared vision. When God's timing is right—we call this a spiritual *kairos* moment—you can seek and secure a new pastor who fits your church's culture, vision, and context.

If you want your church's best days to be in the windshield and not in the rearview mirror, we encourage you to optimize the time of pastoral transition. Seize this opportunity to strengthen your church, and help it soar to new heights of vitality and vibrancy.

Why?

If your church is typical of the church in North America, you might survive a pastoral transition, but you won't thrive. And the reality is your church could cease to exist.

Ouch. We know that hurts.

Long-term, your current facilities may house a different church, apartments, boutique shops, restaurants, or business offices. Or it may be hauled away in a dump truck because the land on which it sits is too valuable to be covered by vacant buildings.

Too harsh? Not really. Parishioners are leaving churches at a greater rate than new people are coming in. Contextual demographics constantly shift, and younger generations exhibit a declining interest in the type of church you were when you were thriving. While it may be the type of church you love, it might not be the type of church that lasts.

The tectonic plates of the church world are shifting, and the resulting earthquakes are jarring Christendom. Like Elijah, churches need to hear and obey the still small voice of God within the noise and distraction of the earthquake, wind, and fire.

We strongly believe churches can soar between pastors, and we are sad when they fail to do so. That is why we wrote this book. Like Jesus, we love the church. We were reconciled to God through Christ, discipled, and called into ministry through the love, care, nurture, and witness of great churches. Recently, I (Tom) returned to the rural church of my youth. In my lifetime, its attendance has declined from 100 to 40. As I drove around my county, I saw church after church either closed or in decline.

Here are our questions for you: 1. Are you ready to accept your church's decline, demise, defeat, and death? 2. Do you really want your church to hang up its cleats and walk off the field? 3. Are you willing to sit passively and allow your church to wane and ultimately die?

The average tenure of a pastor in the typical church is around six years. Yes, there is a small percentage of churches where pastors stay 10, 15, or 20 years or more, but such longevity is more the exception than the rule.

If you are a typical church, this means that about every five years you can reset and start a new journey to soar between pastors. Will you take advantage of these open doors of opportunity? Or will you see the doors close because you are anxious without a pastor and feel an urgency to call a new pastor as quickly as possible?

In some congregations, a pastor's leaving is a negative interruption that may involve conflict or grief. In these situations, it is even more important for the chuch to take the time necessary to thrive during a pastoral transition so that it soars with faith as it moves forward into the tenure of a new pastor.

In situations where a pastor has stayed five to seven years or more before leaving, it is essential that congregations take time to consider where God would have them go. Failure to do so in these situations may harm the ministry of the next pastor.

This book will help you identify the intentional actions to navigate your church through the transition to find and call the P³ Lead Pastor to guide your vision and future. You will find that a pastoral transition can be your church's greatest opportunity to rise to a new level of success. Use today to prepare your church to thrive tomorrow.

Eight Actions

We believe your chance of a fruitful pastoral transition will be greatly enhanced by the eight actions contained in this book, along with the services of an S³ Intentional Interim Pastor.

God has a plan for your church. The past cannot be your future. Embrace these eight actions to ensure that your church's future is God's future. Why would you want anything less?

Here are the eight actions:

Action One—Stabilize the Church or Search for Smooth Air. What are the issues and decisions you need to address during the first 60 days without a pastor? Who will lead the process to address these? How will you use this moment to create a movement that empowers your church to soar between pastors?

Action Two—Eliminate Challenges to Soaring or Confront the Elephants. During the interim between pastors, what are the challenges hindering your church's ability to soar with faith? Who should confront them, and how should they be addressed for the most redemptive and empowering outcome?

Action Three—Strengthen Leadership or Spend Time in the Spiritual Simulator. During the interim between pastors, what leadership capacity issues will be addressed? What actions need to be taken to improve unity and community among leaders in the church? What is your system for identifying, training, and developing leaders on an ongoing basis?

Action Four—Ascend Through Prayer or Climb When You Are on Your Knees. Would your church commit to pray for the interim process and the next pastor for 100 days? Who are the people passionate about the church's God-given future who will form prayer triplets as an exemplary prayer catalyst for the whole church? If a significant prayer process is successful, how do you measure the impact of that process on your church's future?

Action Five—Become a C^3 Church or Soar into the Future. What are the Great Commission Mission, Enduring Core Values, and God's Empowering Vision for your church? Are your leaders ignited by that vision? How well do you reflect the characteristics of the very early Christian Church?

Action Six—Soar with D^3 Intentionality or Align Your Ministry with God's Empowering Vision. How well do your current processes, programs, and ministries (PPMs) align with God's Empowering Vision? How do they intentionally support disciple-making, developing leaders, and dynamic, innovative execution? How will you measure the intentionality, significance, and impact of your disciple-making, developing leaders, and your dynamic, innovative execution?

Action Seven—Call a P^3 Lead Pastor or Continue to Soar Far and High. How would your church define a passionate, proactive, and personable P^3 Lead Pastor for your situation? How does what you have learned as a C^3 Soaring Church seeking to fulfill God's Empowering Vision with D³ Intentionality inform the pastoral search process? What does an excellent P³ Lead Pastoral search process look like? Who are the best people in your church to serve on the Pastoral Search Team (PST)? How will you know when you have found the P³ Lead Pastor for your church?

Action Eight—Engage an S³ Intentional Interim Pastor or Connect with a Sully. Is an S³ Intentional Interim Pastor right for your church? What will it look like to have an S³ Intentional Interim Pastor serving your church? Do you have the desire, patience and assurance of God's leadership to engage in the actions recommended in this book?

Let us get started with Action One now.

Stabilize the Church
Search for Smooth Air

What are the issues and decisions you need to address
during the first 60 days without a pastor?

———

Who will lead the process to address these?

———

How will you use this moment to create a movement
that empowers your church to soar between pastors?

———

On January 15, 2009, US Airways Flight 1549—an Airbus A320—took off from New York's LaGuardia Airport. Sixty seconds into liftoff, the plane struck a skein of geese, killing the engines. Anxiety seized the passengers. Something similar happens to a congregation when a pastor leaves.

When a pastor leaves a church for either positive or negative reasons, anxiety ripples through the church. Passengers and crew of an airplane don't expect to hit a flock of birds; a congregation doesn't expect to lose their pastor. This causes moderate anxiety for some churches, and panic for others, whose members fear they are going to lose their church.

The more turbulent the pastor's departure, the more chaotic the transition. Some churches can adjust and maintain trim through the turbulence while others nosedive.

Whether or not your pastor was beloved, his leaving undoubtedly created great grief and anxiety. Many of your congregants may feel disoriented, perplexed, lost, remorseful or sad, while others are happy the pastor is gone. Not everyone will have the same perspective and feelings. This can create division in your church.

Some members think their problems walked out the door with the departing pastor, while others ask, "Why did he leave? Didn't he love us? Why did God take him away from us? Will we ever find someone as good as our retiring pastor? Who is going to fill in until we get a new pastor? Is this the time for our family to look for another church?"

Others may feel guilt: "Were we too hard on the pastor? Have we become repeat offenders who chew up pastors and spit them out? Does his leaving suggest we have issues to address?"

How a congregation answers these questions reveals a lot about its spiritual and organizational health. How would your church answer these questions? What does it say about the spiritual and organizational health of your church?

No matter what circumstances prompt a pastor's leaving, the church's immediate situation is the same. Uncertainty and urgency require immediate action to reassure members and to find smooth air. A pastor's sudden departure can create a fierce downdraft that can pull your church into a deadly tailspin, especially if you miscalculate your response. Or at least, it will feel that way.

A poorly handled transition carries a high cost. It can lead to membership loss, a decline in attendance, low morale, and a decrease in giving, enthusiasm, effective evangelism, and pastoral care. One church we know dropped from 2,500 to 1,100 because of a poorly handled transition. Sad to say, but these types of experiences occur regularly in churches of all sizes, locations, and denominations.

During a leadership vacuum, a strong personality can take control and move the church toward his or her agenda. Small issues can escalate into a crisis. A poorly handled transition can lead to factions and power struggles. At the very least, it will place your church into a holding pattern. Have you been on a plane with your destination immediately below you, while you circle, waiting for the weather to clear or other aircraft to land? It is frustrating, isn't it? You are so close, yet so far.

This is why you need to have a transition plan in place. You want to make sure you take the right first steps in the first 60 days after your pastor leaves. This will significantly increase your church's ability to call a P^3 Lead Pastor with the potential to have a successful and fruitful ministry.

The first essential action may not feel like the right one. It is natural for church leaders to ask, "What do we do now?" Often leadership moves too quickly with a shortsighted process. A hasty transition can further destabilize a church rather than provide a providential platform for evaluation and forward movement.

The longer it has been since the last pastoral search, the more natural it is to want to do something quickly. Although it seems counterintuitive, the best immediate response is doing nothing—at least in the first hours after learning that you might not have someone to preach this Sunday. It's a good time to practice your belief that God is in control, that Jesus can calm the storm. So, relax. Breathe. Pray without ceasing.

A hasty transition can further destabilize a church rather than provide a providential platform for evaluation and forward movement.

You will find the smooth air of God's presence, peace, and power.

When your leadership gathers, they will need to address the standard decisions required to stabilize a church in the immediate aftermath of a pastor's departure. First, maintain the routines and programs familiar to your congregation. This will help them feel safe and ease their fears.

Second, decide who will assume the preaching duties and help provide pastoral care, administration, and leadership in the short-term while working on a long-term interim plan. You will want a person or persons of experience, confidence, and spiritual maturity whose words and presence will feed the people and reassure an anxious congregation. You will need a wise, experienced leader, guide, and helper who will manifest the S³ Intentional Interim Pastor characteristics of *seasoned, skilled, and strategic.*

Third, your leadership team needs to deal with the big picture of why the pastor left and the circumstances that led to his departure. Be as transparent as possible with the congregation. Share all that you can. Honesty nurtures trust!

Once you have navigated the church out of rougher air, you can breathe easier and realize your church will not crash because your pastor left. Some churches have enough inherent strength to not only fly through the storm but also to evaluate themselves and become stronger than they were before. Many churches, of course, are not as resilient, and some actually make things worse.

If your church is not able to approach this transition as a season of soaring and thriving, it's okay simply to maintain. The goal is to get a church in shape before trying to offer the church to new pastor candidates. You would not attempt to run a marathon without getting a health checkup and a conditioning regimen. You would not try to sell your house without updating it and making repairs. Why would you do any less with the church?

Some churches think they do not need help. However, a healthy church is always under construction. Paul demonstrated this when he planted churches and returned to strengthen them—as we see in Acts 15:3-6. He and his missionary partners laid deeper foundations, resolved problems, admonished, cajoled, encouraged members, and chose leaders. Even perceived healthy churches can profit from an evaluation and actions that will strengthen them.

Is This a Chronos Moment or Kairos Movement?

Hopefully your deepest desire will be to see God turn this experience from a Chronos moment into a Kairos movement that could launch a new spiritual and strategic journey for your church to soar in this in-between time.

We have a myriad of instruments that indicate the passing of Chronos moments, mechanically following nature's time passages: the sun's rise and fall, the seasons moving past our picture windows with green leaves, hot sun, color, and snow.

Unlike Chronos time, a Kairos moment presents a unique opportunitiy for churches to take significant steps forward with God's empowering leadership. A Kairos moment can transform Chronos moments into a movement of soaring and thriving between pastors. The Bible admonishes us in Ephesians 5:15-17 to make the most of the time and take advantage of the moments presented to us.

———

Rather than asking how quickly they can get a new pastor, wise churches should ask, "How can we prepare ourselves to call the right pastor and have a more fruitful future?"

———

The Apostle Paul uses the term Kairos for God's timing. Kairos is translated from ancient Greek as "suitable time" or a "right moment." The pastoral transition can be a Kairos moment or a tipping point that can become a movement to invigorate your church to become even more fruitful. It is a unique opportunity for the church to mount up with strength as an eagle and to soar and not be faint. (See Isaiah 40:28-31). A pastoral transition is an opportunity to ensure your church is firmly founded on the rock and not the sand.

(Matthew 7:24-27) It is a time to discern which platforms are weak, where mortar has loosened around the bricks, what plumbing is leaking in the house that is your church. Do not reject this renewal mindset, and bypass this transition opportunity. The research shows that three-fourths of North American churches are plateaued or declining. If you are in that group, you can take advantage of the opportunity to strengthen your church during transition.

Asking the Right Question

Too many churches want to know how quickly they can get a new pastor.

Here is the answer: For healthier churches, the average time between pastors is 9–15 months. For troubled churches, it is 12–24 months. The longer your pastor was in place, the longer your season of transition needs to be. A church needs an interim for one month for every year a departed pastor served. That might sound too long, but it's necessary to allow the church family the time to grieve their pastor's loss and make the spiritual and emotional adjustments needed to accept and open their hearts to the right pastor for the church's next season.

Rather than asking how quickly they can get a new pastor, wise churches should ask how they can prepare themselves to call the right pastor and have a more fruitful future.

They take advantage of this Kairos moment to engage in a movement to prepare their souls to receive a new pastor and increase fruitfulness upon his arrival. During a healthy transition, the church family makes the spiritual and emotional adjustments that will help them move from the pain of losing their long-term pastor to acceptance and love for their new pastor and family.

How productive do you want your church to be? How fruitful do you believe God wants your church to be? You can grow from no fruit to fruit, from some fruit to more fruit. The pastoral transition is the time to prepare your church for a stronger gospel impact on its members and its community.

"Seize the day!" says Paul in Ephesians 5. You have a moment in time that will not come around again for a while. You are in the most opportune moment to evaluate, correct, and strengthen your church, and prepare it for a brighter future!

Skill and Experience in the Captain's Seat

After Flight 1549's engines were disabled by the bird strike, every second was critical. The aircraft began to lose altitude with impact just a few minutes away. Fortunately, a highly experienced 57-year-old former jet fighter pilot was flying the plane. His name was Chesley "Sully" Sullenberger.

Sully radioed the air traffic tower that he had to make an emergency landing. The air traffic controller gave directions to head toward Teterboro Airport. Sully calmly told them they could not make it. "We're going to be in the Hudson," he exclaimed. Then he instructed the 150 terrified passengers and five crew members to brace for impact. Ditching the plane safely into the Hudson River would take every bit of his experience and skill. But Sully was seasoned, skilled, and strategic. He was a S^3 in flying airplanes.

When your pastor leaves, now or in the future, who will fly the plane with the skill that can only come from experience? Who will perform all the functions of your departed pastor? Who will pilot the church safely and successfully to land so a new pastor can help it soar upward into God's vision for the future?

For your church, that decision can be life or death. It matters who flies the plane. It matters who fills the pastor's shoes. But who?

1. Who Will Preach? Preaching is the most significant perceived and stabilizing benefit a pastor provides a church. A skilled interim preacher will feed your congregants with rich nutrients from God's Word. An experienced preacher will come to know the congregation's needs and preach messages that target those needs. With biblical and targeted messages, the attendees are less prone to leave for a new church. If they are content and spiritually nourished your congregation will more likely trust the pastoral transition to bring them the right pastor. This is a good time for your church to sing the song "In His Time."

2. Who Will Lead the Church and Work with the Leadership Team? Pastoral leadership is needed more than ever when a church is in transition. Without good leadership momentum can slow, and the church begins to lose altitude. Between pastors, someone must inspire the people's

----

*Good leadership during the pastoral transition
tends to attract good pastoral candidates.*

----

confidence, offer wise guidance, work closely with the leadership, and shepherd the flock. Such a leader will also increase your church's spiritual, relational, and organizational health.

Good leadership during the pastoral transition tends to attract good pastoral candidates. But, if your church is simply biding time and not addressing issues or discerning and living into a God-given vision, it will atrophy. The best applicants will go elsewhere, leaving you with second and third-tier pastors. Do you want a pastor that scores of churches have passed over? Your church community, with its Great Commission mandate, deserves the best pastor to feed and lead it.

3. Who Will Guide the Staff? The most challenging and riskiest job for a pastor is ensuring the paid and volunteer staff are unified, focused, and productive. I (Tom) have listened to over 600 churches tell their story of why their pastor left. Many of those recounted how the staff brought the pastor down and sucked the energy out of him until he resigned. By this point the staff is just as demoralized. The needs of the staff are never greater than when a pastor leaves.

During the pastoral transition, the staff and volunteer workers need spiritual and programmatic guidance, supervision, and encouragement. The staff's spiritual, mental, and emotional state permeates the church, affecting its mood and effectiveness. Your associate pastors and ministry directors need someone they like and respect, who takes an interest in them, listens, calms their fears, keeps them on track, and helps them excel at their job. They need someone who can help them prepare for a P^3 Lead Pastor.

When a pastor leaves, hurt and injured staff members need healing. I (Tom) served as an S^3 Intentional Interim Pastor. In four years under their previous pastor, this church's attendance fell from 850 to 430. Their reserve funds had declined from $100,000 to $1,000. They could not pay the bills and impulsively laid off three employees who worked in the church office, creating an uproar in the church. The next week the pastor accepted the call to a new church. The congregation was confused, angry, and divided.

The associate pastor valued the departed pastor, who had taken time to befriend him, build into his life, and treat him like a real colleague. He was hurting and grieving. He had seen 400 people leave in four years, and his pastor had just left.

When I arrived, I recognized the associate pastor's hurt. I immediately went to work, healing and renewing his spirit. Each Tuesday, I bought lunch, and we poured over his life, talked shop, and enjoyed our time together. In return, he regularly had me over for dinner with his wife and two fine boys. I included him in church planning and gave him some important projects. Often, after he led the worship, I publicly thanked him and told him how blessed we were to have him. Over time, he came alive. The spark returned to his eyes, and his passion for the church and ministry blazed again. I am happy to report that he has gone on to have an even more significant ministry career. We stay in touch.

Other times a church will have an unproductive or insubordinate staff member who has drifted into a new theological camp or ministers' network. With a wise and capable interim leader, the governance team can guide that staff member to seek another ministry placement. I have seen this happen many times. Your new pastor will be pleased that the team took this needed action, providing him a clean slate. Can you imagine coming to a new church as pastor, and they have waited for you to clean up the mess? Do it in the transition and let the new pastor start on the right foot.

You will want an interim who can prevent conflict between staff, especially when one or two want to lead the church through the transition—with the lure of becoming the next pastor. Without a supervising pastor, it is not uncommon for maneuvering among staff members to curry favor for their future. Nature abhors a vacuum, and opportunistic staff will naturally try to fill that vacuum by flexing their roles.

The right guide can keep the staff unified, happy, and productive. So, I ask you, who will lead the church staff and assure that they and their programs function well? Who is going to prepare them for their next pastor? With an S³ Intentional Interim Pastor, your church can do more than survive. It can shine and thrive! Dive, survive, or thrive? What will it be? The leadership and the church have big decisions to make.

Four Possible Paths When Filling the Pastor's Roles During the Interim

1. Select a Guest Pastor to Preach: You can secure a preacher or a series of preachers to handle the Sunday sermons and have volunteers or staff pick up as much slack as possible during the interim. A guest preacher can be a retired pastor, a co-vocational minister, a denominational staff person, or a university or seminary professor who lives in the area. If you take this route, you must consider how you will divide pastoral responsibilities among several people.

If you are a multi-staff church, other staff ministers can preach on Sundays and perform their regular duties. However, this extra burden is not easy for them. Be cautious in making this choice. When an associate with full-time responsibilities takes over preaching, he can quickly become overloaded and burdened. Yes, his adrenaline pumps when he stands before the church audience and opens the Word of God. But sermom preparation and delivery can add 20 hours to the 45 to 60 hours a week he is already working in his primary ministry. This will lead to exhaustion, burnout, and skimping on his main job. And his family can suffer.

A warning light: If an associate pastor hints that he would like to be considered for your new pastor position, you should not call him to be your temporary preacher or interim pastor. If you give him the public prominence of preaching and pastoring and he is not selected as your pastor, you will put him in an untenable position. If Pastor or Lead Pastor is his calling, he will have tasted it and will not be satisfied to return to the associate's role. If he is not elected, he will need to exit the church quickly. Once he feels the calling to be lead pastor, affirmed by his ministry as your interim, there is no going back to his previous role. If he feels the pull to pastor a church, he should go ahead and pursue that calling.

From the other side, your new pastor may be uneasy with his associate, who, in practical terms, preceded him in the pastoral role. Where is his heart? His loyalty? What part of the congregation would have preferred the associate over the new pastor? The likelihood of staff paralysis in this situation is high, and before long, the power conflict will seep into staff relationships until it erupts in total dysfunction.

A word of caution: Some churches, often driven by the treasurer, finance team, or trustees will want to take this time to save money and simply go with pulpit supply and add pastoral responsibilities to other staff members. But pulling in and conserving resources, like Scrooge at Christmas, is not the solution. As the old British saying goes, "Don't be a penny wise and a pound foolish."

Pastoral transition is not a time to think of saving money by forgoing a pastor's salary and benefits by having someone come and preach as the church lay leaders muddle through the process of finding the next pastor. How can you maintain momentum if you are replacing your senior pastor with someone who provides just 20 percent of what he was doing? You will also lose momentum if you add the pastor's duties to your other staff members, who already are pulling full loads.

2. Hire a Part-time Traditional Interim Pastor. You can call a part-time interim pastor who preaches on Sunday, spends a couple of days a week on the field to lead staff, and puts out fires.

3. Secure an S³ Intentional Interim Pastor: Every church in transition can benefit from a spiritually and emotionally mature Intentional Interim Pastor who is *seasoned*, *skilled*, and *strategic*. This person can perform all your pastor's duties, and also have processes, tools, and skills to help your church correct, redirect, and reach toward its full Kingdom potential. How do they accomplish this lofty goal?

A. They will conduct "Get to Know You and the

Church" interviews. In a safe and confidential setting, the interviewing pastor asks many questions. Two of the best are: What do you celebrate about our church? What are your concerns about our church?

As the Intentional Interim Pastor listens, he gains insights into the church's emotional, relational, and organizational state. After 30 to 40 congregant active listening interviews, the interim pastor has the church's spiritual, emotional, relational, and organizational pulse. Those interviewed are honored that a leader took the time to listen to their views and perspectives. They frequently walk out of the interview with smiles on their faces saying, "I sure like our interim pastor. Our church is in good hands."

B. They lead a transition team of leaders and key workers to assess overall church health resulting in a diagnosis of church strengths, weaknesses, and problems leading up to recommendations to strengthen the church.

C. They encourage and help the church to follow the recommendations and take actions that will increase church health.

D. They work with leadership and key workers to clarify who the church is (beliefs and values) and discover and live into its God-empowered future (mission and vision). This task must happen before a pastoral search team can be released to secure a pastoral candidate.

E. They coach the pastoral search team to the successful call of a pastor who fits the church.

F. They assist the church in welcoming its new pastor.

The Rest of the Story

Crippled by the bird strike, US Airways Flight 1549, piloted by Sully Sullenberger, flies over the George Washington Bridge and lines up to ditch the plane into the Hudson River. Knuckles are white, and the passengers and crew offer prayers. Moments from impact, flight attendants give final instructions as Sully shouts, "Brace for impact."

Passengers hold their breath as Sully gently feathers the plane into the Hudson's ice-cold waters. The plane bounces, skips, slows, and settles to a rocking halt. With Sully's heroic courage and immense skill, it is a perfect water landing. Passengers exit onto the wings of the bobbing jet while boats race to help. Sully walks up and down the aisle two times to be sure that all are off the plane. Then like a true leader, he is the last one off. All survive!

A National Transportation Safety Board official described it as "the most successful ditching in aviation history." Sullenberger received honor upon honor for his heroic display of skill and composure. A movie, *The Miracle on the Hudson*, was made starring Tom Hanks as Captain "Sully" Sullenberger. Simply amazing. Some would say impossible. Birds brought down an Airbus 320, with 155 lives on board. Because of the calm and measured actions of a 57-year-old former fighter pilot with decades of flying experience and skill, all survived with no serious injuries.

Your church is now or may soon be without a pastor. The natural reflex is to put together a search committee and expediently call a new pastor. We offer you another mindset. How about using the off-season for training, conditioning, and preparing the church for its future? It makes much better sense to take the actions needed to soar between pastors!

How about identifying and taking down barriers that are blocking your church's gospel effectiveness? How about prayerfully and thoughtfully discerning and starting to live into God's empowering vision for your church? Do these things, and you can conduct a pastoral search from a position of strength rather than weakness.

If it all sounds overwhelming, consider an Intentional Interim Pastor to lead you through it. This pastor will lead you on a spiritual and strategic journey culminating in a healthier church and a pastor who fits your congregation. To learn more about the Intentional Interim Pastor and his benefits, fast forward to Action Eight—*Engage an S³ Intentional Interim Pastor* or *You Need a Sully.*

CALL TO ACTION

- Make a list of the top ten issues and decisions you need to focus on during the first 60 days without a pastor.

- Considering your church governance and the current state of spiritual health within your church, determine which persons or leadership teams need to deal with these top ten issues and decisions.

- Begin to prayerfully and strategically consider how your leadership teams can create a movement that empowers your church to soar between pastors.

CALL TO PRAYER

- Pray for your church, its leaders, and clarity of God's leadership for the first 60 days and the days that follow.

- Pray for the pastor who has left your church—for whatever reason—and his family.

- Pray for all the staff, leaders, members, and attendees of your church as they adjust to this transitional season without a pastor.

- Pray that God will lead your church to the best possible S³ Intentional Interim Pastor.

A Healthy Church Gets Stronger During Pastoral Transition

Before the Civil War, Community Church began in a small, southern town—a place with an Americana touch. Today, this family church is in a booming suburb of a burgeoning city and world-renowned tech research center.

A Church's Journey

After a decade of stability and constancy, this deeply connected family church learned that its pastor of 30 years was retiring.

The retiring pastor loved the congregation, and he and his wife felt loved. The retiring pastor also loved preaching relevant and applicable expository messages.

Their family and friends were all local, their daughter and son-in-law led the youth group, and their grandchildren were teenagers in the church. When their long-term pastor announced his retirement at age 73, the church began looking for a new pastor.

The Chapel reached out to Interim Pastor Ministries, and for ten months, I served as their interim pastor.

Upon arriving, the people opened their hearts to my wife and me for several reasons:

1. We learned their names, visited and listened to them in their homes, and prayed with them. Some came for counseling as the preaching of God's word pricked their hearts. I also prayed daily for them as I opened up the church's pictorial directory and interceded for each person.

2. The congregation expressed appreciation for my preaching as I taught a practical series based on my book, *Wonderful Counselor*, which highlights answers to common problems. My second sermon series was from First Timothy, emphasizing how to work with their new pastor.

3. My wife and I spoke very respectfully and openly about the previous pastor and his thirty years' incredible work. We honored them in every way possible.

4. We immersed ourselves in the life of the church. We jumped in and participated by singing in the choir and playing in the orchestra, participating in Awana, Vacation Bible School, joining trips to local ministries, and attending a wide variety of socials.

5. The congregation liked that we enjoyed their community and state. Living in a new part of the country is an adventure.

Look at what the Lord did in ten months:

1. The congregants trusted and praised the Leadership, knowing that an experienced temporary pastor was in the pulpit, church office, and board room.

2. During the transition, the church family made the emotional adjustment from losing the long-term pastor to accepting the new pastor.

3. The church family was strengthened in their beliefs and convictions by the detailed preaching and teaching of God's word.

4. Their prayer meeting went from a handful to over 50 folks meeting to study, pray at tables, and support the church's ministries.

5. The momentum of the services, programs and ministries stayed strong.

6. The church completed the construction of a new educational building which they paid off in two years.

7. They chose a godly younger pastor with a delightful family to be their new Senior Pastor. He and his family were a good fit for the church.

8. The pastoral "baton" was passed from a faithful long-term pastor to a much younger pastor with no membership or attendance loss.

9. The new pastor had a running start.

10. The church is doing well today!

The high point of the ten-month interim was the baptismal service in which several gave their salvation testimonies. The church rejoiced with them.

One young man told of how he was brought up to believe in God but had never attended church. As a university student, he passed a street preacher on campus and noticed how both students and faculty jeered and derided him.

This student was motivated to go home for the weekend and tell his father he wanted to go to church. They visited Community Church, and this young man was saved when I invited those without Christ to trust Him as their Savior.

This salvation story was my fondest memory. I had the opportunity to teach him, and his father, in our new members' class, the basics of the Christian life and start them on the path of discipleship.

Even a healthy church can benefit from an Interim Pastor!

Eliminate Challenges to Soaring

Confront the Elephants

During the interim between pastors, what are
the challenges hindering your church's ability to
soar with faith?

———

Who should confront them, and how should they
be addressed for the most redemptive and
empowering outcome?

———

A
n airplane was experiencing problems in flight
and landed at the nearest airport. The passengers deplaned and after an hour or so, they were
re-boarded. After being seated, one passenger asked the flight
attendant if they had fixed the plane's problem, "No," she
answered, "We just changed pilots."

When a church is going through turbulence and changes
pastors, they often blame the departed pastor, and name a
perceived deficiency. "It was the pastor's fault," they say. "He
was _____ (you fill in the blank)."

Granted, pastors are not perfect, but some churches have
an elephant onboard in the form of complicated issues that
no one wants to talk about, deal with, and resolve. Instead,
the church procrastinates, thinking the elephant is just too

large to deal with.

Does your church have one, or perhaps several difficult issues, stomping like a mad elephant through your church?

- Sometimes leaders are the issue. Often they are too passive or too strong, and fail to pilot the church to discover and live into a God-given empowering vision.
- Possibly the church is growing older and smaller, and no one is concerned.
- Is there unconfessed sin in the church?
- Maybe there is an irate parishioner—also known as a church bully—who must get his or her way.
- Is the church inward-focused, uninterested in reaching out to its community ?
- Does your church have too many old and perhaps dysfunctional programs and committees?
- Is your congregation busy with church work, but failing to do the work of the church?
- Your church says it believes in prayer. Do your leaders actually encourage individual and corporate prayer?
- Are there flocks of gossipers continually striking at the church's unity?
- Is there too much red tape along with cumbersome approval policies to get anything done?

The list can go on and on.

Every church has something, so it is appropriate to ask yourself, are we going to have a failure of nerve and do nothing? Will your leadership kick the can down the church aisle for someone else to handle? Will you let the elephants wreak havoc in your church?

We hope not. For the sake of Christlike ministry in your church, we encourage you to commit to eliminating the challenges to soaring. Too many eternal consequences are at stake to delay on needed action. God is counting on your church to join Him to seek and save the lost and shepherd the found into deepening spiritual maturity.

Unattended issues hinder the fruitfulness of a church and the tenure and effectiveness of pastors. If problems are allowed to fester, they will crush your vitality and vibrancy. Churches can be functional but lifeless, like shrines. If yours is full of religious activity and lacking spiritual vitality it could be that Jesus has not been invited in.

Remember, just as Jesus is knocking on the door of your heart wanting to come in, he is also knocking on the church's door and wants to come in (Rev. 3:19, 20). God speaks to us during disruption and disequilibrium to get our attention. He may be banging on the cabin door and shouting out, "Wake up folks!" It is time for contrite hearts, confession, and repentance that will restore God's favor upon your ministry.

Act Now to Address the Inertia in Your Church

The interim period presents a perfect opportunity to assess and address issues that hinder and hamper churches.

The best way to do so is to secure an S³ Intentional Interim Pastor who has no agenda other than preparing your church for a more vibrant future. An S^3 is someone who can be honest with you about the issues blocking missional engagement and gospel results. Additionally, an S^3 is motivated to get your church in shape to secure a P^3 Lead Pastor.

Former Pastor: An Inhibitor to Church Growth?

Perhaps the pastor was pushing a new building project on the church. Because of the force of his personality or the length of his tenure, no one wanted to disappoint him. Momentum pushed the project forward when in reality most of the congregation did not want to take on the project and pay for its construction and long-term operational costs.

Was the former pastor impersonal? Did his preaching fall short? Did he not take Sabbath rest and succumb to burn out? Did his lack of organizational skills contribute to chaos? Did he have mediocre leadership competencies, unable to develop new leaders? How trustworthy was he? Did people suspect moral failure, emotional issues, a struggling marriage, dishonesty, or mismanagement?

Are any of these descriptors applicable to your former pastor? If so, their departure presents an opportunity for growth.

Consider Lay Leadership Competencies

Your lay leaders may have lacked the leadership competencies to take the church to the next level. Were they responsible for your static state, or is your condition due to a combination of factors? You need to own your issues and make personal and churchwide adjustments, so the next pastor comes into church already soaring with faith and ready to reap an abundant harvest.

Have leaders taken some missteps, made some poor decisions, and lost the congregation's trust? Are the members of

---

Actualizing your vision will help you define key characteristics and values for your church.

---

the leadership team spiritually, emotionally, and relationally immature?

Does your church have a perpetual board that is autocratic and untrained? Is there a mentorship pathway that selects aspiring leaders and grows them into biblical, astute, and wise leaders? Or are board members simply elected by popular vote at a congregational meeting?

Does your leadership team depend on bureaucratic processes more than seeking God's heart and direction? Does the leadership fail to take the time to discern a God-given empowering vision and help the church live into that vision?

Do any of these conditions describe your church's leadership? If so, it's time to change your leadership culture.

Consider Congregational Issues

Maybe the parishioners love to gossip, and tolerate sin in the body. Perhaps they consider Sunday morning attendance the extent of their commitment to God and the church.

Do you have church members who block leaders, and weigh the church down with constant objections to new and innovative ideas? They oppose any change in music or worship style, schedule, program, staffing, or facilities that do not benefit them directly or fit their understanding of how a church ought to function. A few naysayers can prevent you from moving forward.

Do you have an *overly churched culture congregation*, exclusive and content to view Sunday mornings as a weekly family reunion? Do your members fail to pray, hope, reach out to the lost and seek to bring them to Christ and the church?

Do any of these descriptors characterize your members and attendees? If so, you need to change your entire church culture.

Change Begins with a God-Given Empowering Vision

Is the congregation captivated by God's empowering vision for their future? Does the church set challenging faith goals and take calculated risks to reach toward new heights? Your church can't fly, and certainly not soar, if there is no vision. The main job of a leader is to cast a vision, which includes defining that vision and putting it into action.

Maybe your church has a complex and cumbersome church program structure that might ensure short-term success. But without the long-term empowerment of a vision, your church will certainly flounder.

Actualizing your vision will help you define key characteristics and values for your church. Does your church have a disciplemaking process that helps people discover their spiritual gifts and ministry passion? Does your church use these discoveries to coach volunteers toward a ministry that includes both giftedness and passion? When people serve the church using their God-given spiritual gifts, they will be fruitful and fulfilled.

If you have effective discipleship processes in keeping with your vision, your church will likely move forward. This can

---

Your leadership may resist a transparent evaluation for fear of surfacing problems they cannot handle or control. They will be tempted to leave these issues for the new pastor.

---

only happen if you deal with the elephants dragging you down, depleting your energy and resources, and depriving your congregation of the spiritual nourishment they so desperately need.

Unless these church issues are dealt with and resolved, your church's future is compromised and at risk.

Your next pastor will likely be gone within a few years, not because of their shortcomings, but because of the issues the church never resolved.

Still Not Convinced You Need to Confront Your Elephants?

Of the hundreds of churches Interim Pastor Ministries has helped, we have never found one without internal issues. Whatever the issues, we have also found that an S³ Intentional Interim Pastor facilitates problem-solving and helps lead the church on a spiritual and strategic journey to discover and intentionally live into their God-given empowering vision.

So, the question you must ask is this: What are our internal issues? If you conduct an assessment with your members, you are likely to hear them voice many of the following concerns or questions.

- "With the pastor gone, we feel uncertain about our future."
- "Our church body is more divided than we thought."
- "Too many of the decisions we make are politically based, rather than demonstrating a willingness to take a spiritual risk."
- "We need to sell the parsonage."
- "We experienced an immediate power shift when our pastor left as people sought to grab power."
- "Why did the pastor really leave?"
- "Our church is getting older, and younger families are leaving."
- "Why did we let the youth minister go three years ago? We were never given a satisfactory answer."
- "I can't remember the last time we've baptized anyone except children of our church families."
- "I love this church, but something doesn't feel right."
- "I know several families who are thinking about leaving during this interim period, but they will not tell me why."

Members of your congregation may discern a power struggle between leadership teams or between staff members. Strong personalities may be causing conflict among members with the real threat of a split. People may be angry because a few people are controlling the church. In a time of crisis other issues can become magnified and normal practices questioned, such as finances, contributions to the denomination, and missionary support.

Your leadership may resist a transparent evaluation for fear of surfacing problems they cannot handle or control. They will be tempted to leave these issues for the new pastor. If not dealt with, they will continue to foster discontent and can lead to a rough flight and a short tenure for the next pastor.

My (George) father served as an interim pastor following his retirement from a long-term ministry position. He told me about some elephants in a church he was serving. I asked him if he was going to document these for the new pastor to address. "No," he said. "I'll deal with them so the next pastor won't have to. I think he'll appreciate that!"

A few years later, I got to know the pastor called to the church where my father had served as the interim. I told him about the conversation with my father. He told me how much he appreciated what my father had done because it allowed him to immediately begin moving the church forward without having to deal with a cluster of carry-over problems.

I (Tom) know a church that was between pastors and enduring a toxic pastoral staff. The leaders agreed that the whole pastoral team needed firing. Yet, during the interim period, they did nothing. The new pastor inherited these troublemakers who had a support base more substantial than his. His tenure lasted only a year as the staff undermined his leadership.

Companies, marriages and churches derail because people are afraid to confront reality. They pretend to not see the problems, the elephants in the room, hoping they will miraculously go away. They won't.

What's needed is robust and unbridled conversation that encourages people to come out from behind themselves, to say what they are really thinking. Most people want to hear

---

Whatever the reason your pastor left, not everyone is sad. No pastor has a 100 percent approval rating.

---

the truth even if its uncomfortable. The truth can only set you free if you first identify it, including the truth of a situation that might be choking your church. This is followed by the truth of what must be done.

If you don't do this, your new pastor doesn't have a chance. He will step into the seat of an airplane whose instruments are failing.

Planes fly safely only when they undergo regular inspections and maintenance. Logbooks that stay with the aircraft show everything that has been done to the plane, including where and by whom. They leave nothing to chance, and even then, at times, systems can fail them because an issue that had gone undetected suddenly manifests during the stress of flight.

Churches are organic systems, and are susceptible to disease just as people are. Undiagnosed, these diseases can become silent killers of people and of churches. Churches need regular inspections and maintenance. They also need regular and special times of spiritual discernment and in-depth assessment of the church systems. One of the best times to do this review is the season between pastors.

The transition between pastors presents a golden opportunity to recognize and deal with the elephants in the church systems, to remove barriers to health, growth, and vital ministry. Your church can then regroup, renew relationships, address organizational needs, discover your God-given empowering vision, and call the next pastor to lead you into a fruitful future. All this puts your church on a trajectory toward more excellent gospel ministry and effectiveness.

So, deal with your issues. Lighten the load. Throw your excess baggage onto the tarmac. Clear the runway.

Take off and soar into God's future for your church. Chart this course and your best days will be ahead of you.

The Most Obvious Elephant Is the Pastor's Departure

Whatever the reason your pastor left, not everyone is sad. No pastor has a 100 percent approval rating. Some of the disapproving members who were adversaries of the pastor remain in the church. They believe the church was more theirs than his, and they were determined to outlast him.

There is rarely unanimous agreement that a pastor's

departure was the best option for the church. No matter what the circumstances were. A significant number of members might have joined the church during this pastor's tenure. While it might be an overstatement to say they joined *because* of the pastor, we recognize that unique pastoral qualities often attract a unique set of people. These people may be more upset than others that he left.

We need to own our problems and address them, as well as recommit to personal discipleship and healthy church ministry so that the next pastor comes to a church already in motion. He should not be expected to revive the church. We want him to be excited about helping us fulfill our God-given empowering vision for the church's future and bringing new and innovative ideas for how we might fulfill that vision.

Friction Can Result in a Smooth Flight

You can't move without creating friction. Motion produces friction which in turn provides movement.

Flight is friction. Fast flowing air colliding with the wing creates lift and helps move an airplane foreward. Churches will not ascend to new heights without encountering some resistance and creating friction in the transition period. Change cannot happen without conflict. Churches can only grow when they embrace conflict.

Firing a mismatched staff member or confronting a bully board member creates tension especially when they have the support of people within the church. The friction this creates is never comfortable, but it's necessary for the church to soar to new heights. Issues need to be addressed and people need to be dealt with.

Whenever a church advances God's vision, there will be friction. Not everyone is willing to embrace the changes prompted by that vision. Yet we must remember there is no movement without proactive actions that both create friction and arise from it.

As in flight, so in the church, nothing moves without friction.

A businessman who attends the church overcomes his anxiety and meets with the elders about a problem he sees.

A pastor sits down with a young couple from his church and tells them that living together is sinful and contrary to God's Word.

A church member shares Christ with a neighbor, who takes offense and shuns her.

The leadership reprimands an associate pastor for breaking confidences and trust.

It takes courage to act.

Do not fear the elephant. Rather, face the elephant. Point it out, rope it, tame it, or lead it out the door into the wild.

Achieving greater positives usually requires enduring lesser negatives. Get the greater by addressing the lesser.

Leadership Transparency During the Interim Is Vital

The lay leadership of the church must be as transparent as possible during the interim between pastors. You do not want your members to be anxious, not knowing why the pastor

High-performance pastors seek churches that are already in motion and ready to be led by a pastor who wants to lead a church committed to God's Great Commission and Great Commandment.

left suddenly. Controlling communication leads to speculation and often damages the reputation of both the departed pastor and the church leadership. While knowledge is power, you do not need to seek or keep such power. The congregation wants and needs to trust its leadership.

A key strategy is for the lay leadership to appoint a person as spokesperson who will relay all official communication during the interim—especially until an interim pastor is secured. At that point, lay leadership and the interim pastor can negotiate the spokesperson's role.

If too many people speak as spokespersons, messages can get confusing and are more likely to represent various personal viewpoints instead of the official viewpoint. Also, the leadership may want to share some information later when they have developed a clear plan for addressing the response to the information.

Answer questions frankly and as entirely as you can without embellishing. Do not jump on the rumor mill, or hazard guesses. "I don't know" is a legitimate answer if you do not know. People will want to know what prompted a pastor's leaving, especially if it's not to another ministry opportunity.

If there are legal issues involved, of course, you must be

aware and respectful of the restrictions such a challenge imposes. At the same time, you want to create trust. Trust relieves anxiety. Trust inoculates the congregation from stress. Every leadership action will be better received when the flock trusts its shepherd leaders.

Hold on a Minute—Don't Rush to Takeoff!

Even if you believe your church is doing ok, do not rush. Take time to discern God's leading, God's timing, and God's next pastor for your church. Do not be like the typical col- lege football team who within weeks of losing their coach hires a new one. Wait for God's open door.

Too often a church's default position is to get a new pastor as quickly as it can. The leadership board of one church took it upon themselves to fire the pastor in his office. They then turned to a seminary intern in an adjoining office and called on him to accept the pastor's role immediately. "You're train- ing to be a pastor," said the board chair. "You can be ours starting right now."

Of course, that young pastor did not last long. Don't become the church of the revolving door, with pastors com- ing and going. If so, the pool of excellent pastoral candidates will quickly diminish until there are none.

Generally speaking, there are more ordained persons in many denominational families who want to serve as pastor of a church or move from the church they currently serve than churches to be served. You will not lack prospects.

Your church must become the best church before it can

call the best pastor. Healthy churches call healthy pastors. Less healthy churches call less healthy pastors.

Your church thinks it is 100 percent healthy, yet even healthy churches are always under construction. Every church must push toward the mark of God's high calling (Phil. 3:13-14).

With the right interim leadership, churches can always improve their health during the transition between pastors.

Pastors who want—and have the capacity—to take churches to new heights are looking for churches already aspiring to those heights. High-performance pastors seek churches that are already in motion and ready to be led by a pastor who wants to lead a church committed to God's Great Commission and Great Commandment.

Affirm and Build On Your Strengths

Confronting and dealing with problems in the church is always easier if you also continually remind the congregation of its strengths. Affirming them provides a huge boost to morale.

Consider and celebrate such things as your church's history and accomplishments, your loving congregation, your neighborhood's opportunities, and your church's faithful giving. Do something public to affirm what is good, right, and loving about the church and build on its strengths.

Simply confronting challenges will not enable your church to soar between pastors. Kennon Callahan, author of *Twelve Keys to an Effective Church*, told me (George) numerous times that you can fix everything that is wrong, weak, or challenging in a church and bring it up only to neutral.

Fixing what's wrong will clear the runway, but will not empower a church to take off and soar. Focus on what's right with your church. Leverage its strengths to help it take flight. Use your strengths to address the areas of weakness.

In the next section we will suggest ways to affirm and build on your strengths. But first, here are some ways you can affirm your congregation.

Stories of remembrance.

- Remember the ten kids that got saved at a youth camp and baptized the next Sunday.
- Recall the family that responded to God's call to be missionaries in Southeast Asia.
- Tell afresh the story of God's financial faithfulness when your church experienced an economic downturn after the nearby military base closed, or during the pandemic.

Focus on the positives.

- Your programming continues as before.
- Volunteers are in place who love the church and the people involved in their programs.
- Your mission and vision are discovered and activated anew.
- Perhaps you have the area's most successful youth ministry or weekday preschool or music program, etc.
- Or you are very involved in your local schools through teacher appreciation, reading buddies, and providing

weekend food backpacks.

- You are recognized as a strong worshipping community.
- Your church is prominently visible on a major thoroughfare, with thousands of cars going by each day.

Do not hesitate to affirm and build on your church's strengths. Your members are aware that this is a critical transition for your church, and they want to find the best pastor, called by God, to be their next leader. They are anxious for a bright future and expectantly hopeful for it.

Proactively Confront the Elephants in the Church

How can leadership proactively confront the elephants in the church? In Action Four, we offer a powerful dialogue, prayer, and discernment initiative. For now, we would like to suggest some questions and tools for you to consider.

Ongoing dialogue with the church participants—the congregation—is important at the beginning and throughout the interim process. In group settings, raise core conversations and dialogue, which can continue throughout the interim period. Here are some suggested conversation starters:

Exercise One: Top Ten Signs of Health and Strength in the Life and Ministry of Your Church

1. Do this exercise within the first sixty days after the pastor is no longer serving as pastor.
2. Have a congregational-wide event and urge everyone to attend.

3. Seat people around tables of six to eight.

4. Provide each person with a sheet of paper with this question at the top, "What are the Top Ten Signs of Health and Strength in the Life and Ministry of Our Church During the Past Twelve Months?"

5. The sheet should provide spaces to list ten things.

6. Ask each person—without talking to their neighbor—to write down the first ten things that come to mind, such as events, programs, experiences in groups, and church participants' qualities and characteristics.

7. After a few minutes, have the people at each table discuss what they wrote down, and then come up with a top ten list for their table.

8. Note: The top ten lists do not need to be in priority order. They simply need to be ten things around which the table group develops a consensus.

9. Have a representative of each table stand up and read their list of ten things—even if someone before them said some of the same things.

10. Each table's consensus lists are then handed in and tallied to discover the ten items mentioned.

11. These top ten signs of health and strength indicate the church's key perceived foundational strengths.

Exercise Two: Discovery of Hopes and Dreams for the Future of the Church

1. Conduct 90-minute group interviews with approximately a dozen congregants plus a moderator and recorder.

2. Conduct as many interviews as you desire, with a minimum total attendance of at least 25 percent of the typical weekly worship attendance. The higher the percentage the more invested your congregation will be in this process.

3. Provide a written questionnaire that people can complete in writing and hand in at the end of the group interviews. They do not need to place their name on the form.

4. Here are suggested questions. The facilitator can add more church-specific questions.

   • What are signs or indicators of health and strength in the life and ministry of our church? Where should we be rejoicing in the Lord about how our church is doing?

   • What are signs or indicators of challenges and concerns in the life and ministry of our church? Where should we be lamenting and mourning with the Lord about how our church is doing?

   • What are some of our hopes and dreams about the future ministry of our church? What excites us about the future of our church? What indicators reflect God's empowering vision for the future of our church?

   • What are any barriers or obstacles that may prevent us from ministering and serving in significant ways in response to God's empowering vision for our church? How do we best address these barriers or obstacles?

Beyond these two exercises, you may also want to reach out to your denominational office for any processes or tools to help assess your current situation and project God's future for your church.

I (Tom) value the Natural Church Development (NCD) assessment tool, built around eight healthy church characteristics. You can obtain information about this tool at *https:// ncdamerica.andrews.edu/store.*

Another assessment tool is CHAT (Church Health Assessment Tool), which has 12 church health characteristics and will score your church on each component. *https://www. healthychurch.net*

Interim Pastor Ministries also has a proprietary diagnostic tool called Ministry Insight Tool (MIT) available to the churches they serve. This tool helps your church affirm its strengths while addressing the elephants in the room.

Another approach is to engage an experienced S^3 Intentional Interim Pastor with many church health diagnostics tools to help your church gain a clear picture of the church's strengths and weaknesses. Interim Pastor Ministries has pastors who are skilled in administering church health assessments.

If your church needs to understand the friction and conflict you have, I (George) would recommend my book *Every Congregation Needs a Little Conflict* (Chalice Press, 2008) as a great resource to determine the intensity level of conflict and the best way to confront those elephants.

CALL TO ACTION

• Identify and address the challenges to your church's ability to soar with faith during the interim period.

• Determine who should address these challenges for the most redemptive and empowering outcome.

CALL TO PRAYER

• Pray that your church, its leaders, and members will have the courage to confront these issues.

• Pray for those in your church family who mourn the loss of your pastor. It is real for them and should not be ignored or dismissed.

• Pray for the people who are glad the pastor is gone. Unless they confront their own feelings and actions, they may carry these over to the next pastor.

Safari of Grace Corrals an Elephant in the Room

I came to Sonrise Church several months after the lead pastor had resigned under pressure, leaving behind a congregation burdened with strained and unreconciled relationships. Realizing that God's word heals, I preached sermons on the graces of confession, forgiveness, teachability, confrontation, and reconciliation. God moved and church members approached one another with transparent vulnerability, asking and seeking forgiveness. By God's grace hard feelings left and joy returned. But there was an elephant in the room. The congregation was on the "outs" with the departed pastor.

One night I asked our transition team, "How will our experience with Pastor John adversely affect our next season of ministry?" After a pregnant silence, they began to share, one by one, the pain, guilt, and heartache of a broken relationship with their former pastor.

In the days that followed, the group determined to invite Pastor John back to meet with the leaders and core congregational members. Their purpose was to "apply grace to their past."

When they invited Pastor John back, they listed four goals for his visit: (1) Confess that they dishonored him and ask his forgiveness, (2) Assure him that through grace, the church forgave him for any offenses real or perceived, (3) Bless and thank him for his faithfulness to their church, (4) Seek his advice on how they can improve their ability to honor and learn from their next pastor.

In a "pre-meeting" with members, we gathered around a cross on the church grounds. There we remembered what Jesus accomplished on the cross and how He had forgiven all of our sins.

We asked ourselves, "In light of all that God has forgiven

us, how can we withhold forgiveness from John?" Then, one by one, we burned our lists of grievances in a large metal container as "a symbol of forgiveness." In the end, there were ashes in that container, but nothing remained of the words we had written. The ashes reminded us that we had a clean slate through the cross, and we wanted to offer that clean slate of forgiveness to Pastor John. I reminded them that when we met with Pastor John, God would take those ashes, forgive our sins, and remember them no more.

In our meeting with the former pastor and his wife, we sat in a circle. Each person shared specific ways they had failed to honor John and then asked for and received his forgiveness. John acknowledged his offenses, and we forgave him.

John and his wife sat in the center of the circle as, one-by-one, each person stood behind them and blessed them. We witnessed amazing exchanges of reconciliation and healing. All sensed we were applying grace to our past and were ready to move forward as God's people.

An email from John a week later gave me a glimpse of how God used this moment to jnfuse life into John. He wrote, "I wish I had the words to thank you for how gracious, kind, affirming, encouraging, helpful, warm, and forgiving you were. You have all been so kind, forgiving, and gracious to me. I feel that I am so much further ahead in allowing God to continue using me."

God used this process to prepare us for "Pastor Next" and encouraged Pastor John to minister, unencumbered by the past, in the new place where God led him. Grace does that! Grace is more prominent than an elephant!

Safaris of grace corral elephants and lead them out of the room!

Strengthen Leadership
Spend Time in
the Spiritual Simulator

During the interim between pastors, what are the
leadership capacity issues that need to be addressed?

—

What actions need to be taken to improve unity
and community among leaders in the church?

—

What is your system for identifying, training, and
developing leaders on an ongoing basis?

—

A few years ago, I (Tom) traveled to Memphis to visit a church with an IPM Intentional Interim Pastor. While there, a FedEx pilot and flight instructor took the interim pastor and me to the Memphis airport to fly a 30-million-dollar Boeing 777 Flight Simulator.

I did well in the Captain's seat, taking off and landing, until we tried a landing in Hong Kong. Hong Kong's mountainous approach required skill far beyond my one hour of training. I crashed into Hong Kong Bay. The plane skipped across the water, hit land, and exploded. The simulation help me appreciate the intense and rigorous training pilots undergo to fly real 400 million dollar airplanes.

Churches do a reasonably good job of recruiting leadership newbies but do poorly at leadership training and development. This grieves me. The church rises and falls based on its leadership. Leadership can either advance or hinder the mission that Jesus gave to His Church. In these days of unprecedented gospel opportunity, we face a leadership crisis in the church. We need more and better leaders.

We need to train and develop pastors before they serve. We need spiritually mature leaders committed to fulfilling the Great Commission in the spirit of the Great Commandment. While there are "natural born leaders," they will not become good leaders without developing the skills that can only come from rigorous training, modeling, practice, evaluation, and encouragement.

I believe most leadership team members are good people. They love the Lord and His Church. They want to do right. But leadership teams can lose their way, become ineffective, and sometimes function outside God's will. The time between pastors is the time to face leadership team issues and strengthen the team to join hands with the new pastor and lead the church into God's empowering future.

Serving as a church leader is not easy. Your leadership team, whatever you call them—board, council, session, elders, team—carries many weighty responsibilities and functions. They must model spiritual and emotional maturity, build a community among themselves to tackle church issues, keep the church moving forward, lead in vision discovery and fulfillment, set overall policies, put out fires, and work in tandem with the pastor.

They steer the church through smooth, choppy, and

turbulent air. Being a servant leader is hard work, as described by the Greek word for servant or deacon, which literally means "go through the dust." Your soul will get soiled along the way.

Leaders spend many hours in meetings, doing tasks, responding to emails and text messages, and taking telephone calls from people who are not always happy. Leaders encounter obstinate and unappreciative people questioning or blaming them for an unpopular decisions. Periodically leaders get praise from a compassionate person.

When church problems crop up, church board members step up. Under pressure, I have seen leadership teams meet weekly and talk daily. Leading is a heavy responsibility.

In one church where I (Tom) was as interim pastor, the church's complications drove the previous elder chair into an emotional breakdown and hospital stay. He paid a high price for serving a conflicted church.

The weight of leadership is never heavier than during a pastoral transition. Alone without a pastor, lay leaders must create and communicate a transition plan and next steps. If there are challenges, they must solve them. In partnership with the pastoral search team, they must guide the search process to ensure they call the right pastor.

A slip-up in any of these responsibilities can hinder the transition process. One misstep can be devastating. I have seen churches lose speed and altitude during the interim. The time between pastors presents great opportunity as well as risk. The leadership must be effective. They must get it right. They must help the church soar.

I (Tom) served as an interim pastor some years ago in a church that crashed, tearing the fuselage in half, and throwing out one-half of the congregation. Strong personalities intensified a deep divide over tradition and evangelism. One side wanted to preserve the church's heritage while the other side wanted the church to be more outward focused. Even the elders had different perspectives on mundane day-to-day

---

A church with two philosophies of ministry is a church divided. It's a church with double vision, making it impossible to see clearly the path ahead.

---

operations as well as the church's vision. A church with two philosophies of ministry is a church divided. It's a church with double vision, making it impossible to see clearly the path ahead.

As an S³ Intentional Interim Pastor, I labored for an entire year to bring the two factions together by putting together a transition team of elders, deacons, teachers, department heads, and key influencers to get everyone on the same page. Ultimately, we worked to bring the church together with a shared vision and ministry plan. It all came down to a vote on constitutional changes that amounted to a litmus test. Would the church focus on reaching the community for Christ or remain a stable and traditional ministry? The changes required a 70 percent affirmation to pass. We came up three votes short, and one half walked away and formed a new church.

The next Sunday, I stood up to a half-empty worship center and had the most miserable preaching experience of my life. I was distraught that my year of work was for nothing, and I must admit I felt some anger toward those who thwarted progress. As I preached, I was depressed and felt dead inside. Needless, to say, I would not have won a preaching award for that sermon.

The Dilemma for Leadership Teams

Many leadership teams are inadequate to lead a church through a pastoral transition. Yet, because of the mantle of responsibility they wear, they may assume that it is their lot to grit their teeth, bear down, and make something happen.

As counterintuitive as it may seem, the interim is a period when leadership teams can be strengthened to grow together and equip them to guide the church through transition. Yet, few churches have a mentorship program to develop biblically qualified board candidates.

There are no covenants or job descriptions for many leaders. They are recruited and told that their group meets down the hall, the third door on the left. Church leaders often serve because someone must do it, and they feel it's their turn. This is leadership by necessity that does not stir a person's deepest desire to serve, and summon them to the noble calling of leadership (1 Timothy).

While there are many ways to develop and strengthen existing leadership during transition, I recommend having an S³ Intentional Interim Pastor who will live and work among you and create a natural learning environment for your leadership. Your team members will have the opportunity to listen, watch, and learn as your interim pastor resolves conflict, brings order into chaos, listens, and responds to and loves your people. The team will join him in leading diverse elements of your church to bring consensus.

Simply put, an S³ Intentional Interim Pastor, will give guidance and leadership. He will have in his toolkit a clear understanding of how a board can address its issues. If the interim pastor can leave behind a resourced, unified church leadership team, he has accomplished an excellent service for the church and the next pastor.

In one church Interim Pastor Ministries served, the elder chair was a former marine, a bully the others could not face down. The other leaders tolerated his behavior to the point they became unaware they needed to face him down to prevent his fringe ideas from controlling the church's direction. This bullying behavior and subsequent clashes exhausted the previous pastor and caused him to move on. Soon after the interim pastor arrived, the bully took a job transfer out of the area. It seemed a timely resolution. Disciplining him would have been difficult. As soon as he left the leadership united, and the church grew under the interim pastor and successfully called their next pastor.

Consider how your leaders might deal with the following situations that arose in several different churches.

A popular pastor and renowned Bible teacher had a secret life of adultery. He had several intimate affairs and became bold enough to proposition his secretary. Just before their first planned tryst, the pastor was working in the yard and fell over dead. The church called an interim pastor, after which the leadership learned of their former pastor's duplicitous life. What should they do with this shocking revelation? Tell the grieving widow? Tell the church? What would you have done?

How would your church leadership deal with a worship leader who could not sing on pitch and was merely average on the guitar? How would your board approach transitioning the worship leader to a backup position without offending his wife, the part-time children's pastor?

A small-town, historic church called a recent seminary graduate as their pastor. Many said he was the best preacher they had ever heard. The pastor, who was young and had a lovely family, attracted many millennials to the church. The church started growing, as did a division between the staff. Soon the attendance doubled to more than 100. Realizing they needed more space, the church bought land on the edge of town and built a new building. The church flourished, growing from 200 people to 1,000 within two years.

The church then called a young man home from the mission field to be their student pastor. His father was chair of the leadership board. The triangulated leadership dynamics became complex and testy. The pastor and the student pastor often butted heads. When the student pastor resigned, the pastor took so much heat that he left also. A few families, as well as board members, coalesced around the former youth pastor when he expressed interest in becoming the pastor.

Other families knew he would be a disaster for the church. What does leadership do? Do they bring back the former pastor? Who is going to help them solve this problem? How will the church heal?

Does your board have the emotional, spiritual strength and leadership capacity to address such issues during the interim season and afterward? The right interim pastor can help the board address and resolve such issues.

Building Community

Leadership teams are often a conglomeration of opinionated, self-convinced individuals rather than a community of faithful, effective, and innovative leaders. The first group is merely a gathering of egos, the second a true leadership community that you must build.

An important aspect of building community is idenifying controllers. An S³ Intentional Interim Pastor has been trained to identify controllers—people who often ramrod their preferences. These controllers operate through sheer force of personality and conviction that their view is the only one with merit. They are not automatically wrong, but others in leadership need to learn how to stand up for what is right.

More important is your ability to identify capable, biblically qualified leaders who will help guide and shepherd a church, foster unity and develop missional effectiveness. Such leaders do more than meet monthly to do the work of elders, deacons, or council members. They also meet periodically to pray, deepen fellowship, and develop stronger emotional connections. They are friends and ministry colleagues. They grow in character, competency, and capacity. People respect them and feel blessed to have such persons as their leaders.

The stress that inevitably comes with leadership will reveal the character and competency of team members. An excellent interim pastor will develop a consensus strategy and work closely with the leadership team.

Evaluating Your Leadership Team

How do you evaluate the effectiveness of your church leadership team? How do they assess themselves? The interim period is a good time to make changes in the way you choose team members, structure the team, and identify and mentor potential future leaders. Here are some criteria to evaluate present and future board leaders. Use these ten leadership characteristics to assess your team.

Ten Leadership Characteristics

1. Godliness: Leadership team members must be spiritually born again and show spiritual and emotional maturity, honesty, and integrity. They must love Jesus and His Church, be humble and ask forgiveness when they are wrong. It is important they understand more than just their giftedness and their calling; they should also know their identity in Christ. Their effectivenss flows out of the security of knowing who God made them to be and what He has asked them to do.

Leadership teams are often a conglomeration of opinionated, self-convinced individuals rather than a community of faithful, effective, and innovative leaders. The first group is merely a gathering of egos, the second a true leadership community that you must build.

In my first interim ministry, I (Tom) was in a very conflicted church. Soon, the target was on my back. One of the deacons came into my office and got into my face. I teared up. To keep the confrontation from escalating, I walked away. Twenty years later, this former board member wrote to apologize to me. He said, "I was too full of myself; please forgive me." I wrote back and told him that I forgave him and wished him well. It takes a Christlike person to humble themselves and say, "I was wrong; will you forgive me?" Godly leaders look at their shortcomings and lack of holiness, and own their issues. They take responsibility. Does your church have biblical, godly standards for its leadership?

2. Faith: Speaker Les Brown says it well: "Too many of us are not living our dreams because we live our fears." Making fear-based decisions is true of churches as well as individuals. Do your leadership team and church demonstrate faith or fear? If leaders don't step out in faith, their church won't take flight. Leaders should walk by faith rather than by sight in the spirit of 2 Corinthians 5:7. I (George) call these leaders Faith Soaring Leaders.

3. Unity: Unity of the Spirit is essential for the leadership team. God entrusts the team to discern His will and to know the mind of Christ. That is impossible if there is disunity. When there is an oppositional thinker (odd man out), the team needs to confront that person. If a confrontation does not help, call in outside assistance. At the same time, the board must respect differences. Disunity isn't caused by a diversity of viewpoints, but by objectionable behavior.

Members of the board must not operate in secrecy among themselves or be secretive with the congregation. The unity of the Spirit requires getting to know one another. We must go beyond superficial relationships, listen to, seek to understand and learn from one another. Become friends. Great leadership teams build a community to reach a community!

4. Power: Leaders exercise power, and they must use it properly. Determine and communicate a clear, church-wide understanding of who can make what decisions. What are the decision-making powers of the lead pastor? The leadership teams? The congregation?

Dysfunctional leadership allows a few to control the team and make all the decisions. The other members are intimidated by the controllers. They are afraid to assert themselves. Controllers harm the team and, ultimately, the church.

Stop any abuse of power. Clarify and define roles and

———

Good fences make good friends. Team members need to stay on their own turf and not cross over the decision-making fences.

———

positions and the authority that comes with each. When everyone understands their decision-making power and boundaries they work in harmony and minimize conflict. Good fences make good friends. Team members need to stay on their own turf and not cross over the decision-making fences.

5. Communication: People are down on what they are not up on, so communicate, communicate, and then communicate some more. Have a clear communication plan that uses various tools to keep the congregation informed: print, verbal, digital, and personal communication. People hear best with a variety of communication channels.

As appropriate, ask your congregation's opinion on pending decisions and directions, especially if it will affect the entire group. Send out good news communications from the leadership team and keep the church's mission and vision before the people. Give progress reports. One interim pastor sends the whole church an email each week. He is quite honest about what he is discovering and the way forward. He couples this guidance with pastoral care and wise leadership.

6. Focus: Sometimes, leadership teams get lost in the weeds. They micromanage the church rather than delegating day-to-day management and household issues to volunteer or paid staff. The primary responsibilities of a church leadership team are the following:

- **Dependence:** Practicing and modeling God-reliant prayer.
- **Doctrine:** Maintaining sound biblical beliefs.
- **Direction:** Leading the church in discerning and living into a God-given future.
- **Delegation:** Delegating to pastoral and volunteer staff the administration of the church.
- **Discipline:** Dealing with difficult and sinful people.
- **Deployment:** Ensuring the believers are equipped to do the work of ministry in light of their spiritual gifts and passions (Eph. 4:11-16).
- **Dollars:** Providing final fiduciary oversight of the church's finances.
- **Defense:** Protecting the pastor and staff from disrespect, gossip, attack, and church bullies.

7. Peacemaking: Know and practice essential peacemaking skills. So many of the challenges in churches are people oriented. Amid conflict, leaders must have a non-anxious presence. They must respond and not react. To settle disputes, board members need to know and practice peacemaking methodologies. To learn peacemaking skills, we recommend your board study and discuss *The Peacemaker* by Ken Sande. Also, your leaders can contact Ken's organization and schedule a weekend seminar.

8. Size: Leadership teams are often too large and meet for too long. You do not need a lot of members, but you need the right members. Seven to nine is a good number. They should be willing to meet at least ten times a year.

9. Biblical Standards: Leadership must determine proper measurements. Dysfunctional board members bring a corporate mindset to the church board that considers cost or return on investment before considering mission priorities and opportunities. Leadership teams can learn a lot from smoothly operating boards of other entities. However, a corporate mindset can push out biblical values, especially in recent years, as the idea of the pastor as CEO has seeped into church culture.

The church is unlike any secular business or non-profit. The church's mandate is not to create profit for shareholders but to follow the Lord and scripture to fulfill the mission laid out for us. Leadership team members are to be godly shepherds, not simply corporate directors.

Pay attention to these biblical markers of success: How is our church doing to win and make disciples? Are we hearing stories of Jesus changing lives in our midst? Is there an ever-deepening love for Jesus and others in our church? Do we intentionally reach out to the lost, the least, and the last? How are we doing in baptisms and public professions of faith?

Board culture and behavior must be informed and evaluated by the fruit of the Spirit found in Galatians 5:22-23. Wil Regier, a vision clarity coach for churches and formerly a principal administrator for an aerospace company, said it best: "The Spirit of God in church board meetings was something I never experienced with my company. Those experiences with the Holy Spirit were extraordinary moments."

10. Qualify: Healthy church leadership teams develop standards and processes to qualify, train, and develop potential leadership candidates. Be sure that only those who demonstrate godliness, meet the biblical standards as set for in I Timothy and Titus, and have wise and practical leadership skills are nominated and elected. Beware of those who desire to serve on the leadership team who have personal agendas that might conflict with the church's mission.

The best time to fire is before you hire. Guard the gate to the leadership team. It is trite but true that *the cream rises to the top!* Therefore, you should have in place—or create—a process to identify, qualify, train, and develop new leaders with potential.

Consider the training pilots undergo to become captains on a Boeing 777 airplane as referenced in the illustration at the beginning of this chapter. Your leaders need similarly rigorous training. At this point, the urgent task is to be sure you have on your leadership team people trained in these skills. If you do not have these skilled leaders, develop a pipeline through which future leadership team members can be identified, cultivated, enlisted, and trained.

An S³ Intentional Interim Pastor can help your church place an effective leadership team that will vastly improve your chances of finding and calling God's man to be your next pastor. Making such changes is never easy, but it is necessary if your ministry is to go forward. An ineffective board will always hinder progress.

The Leadership Scorecard

On a scale of 1 (low) to 10 (high), have each team member grade the team on the ten leadership characteristics previously stated. Then have each team member share their score and reason for assigning these scores.

It may be helpful to have an outside denominational leader, a consultant, or an S³ Intentional Interim Pastor lead this activity. An unbiased outsider can help the team define the leadership team's health, and recommend further training.

Spend time in the Spiritual Simulator so your team members can deepen their relationship with Christ and develop Godly attitudes and actions.

Optional: You may also want to do this exercise with a broader group of people within your church. It helps if the congregation perceives the gifts and graces of their leadership.

Further Thoughts

In some larger churches, leaders work behind closed doors, and members may not know who they are. Find ways to get your leaders before the people. Introduce them to the congregation. Encourage your leaders to participate, as they are gifted, in the weekend services. For example, some churches' core lay leaders read Scripture and lead a congregational prayer during worship.

Some big churches, for fear of looking unprofessional and "folksy", keep lay leaders away from the pulpit. That is an unhealthy perspective and bad practice. It contributes to the disconnect between leadership and the congregation. With training and practice, your lay leaders can serve as counselors at the front of your sanctuary when people come foreward for prayer or make public decisions for Christ.

You can also use short video introductions, digital and print newsletters, the church's website, and social media to identify and introduce the leadership team. Periodic town hall gatherings will also increase interaction, develop familiarity and build trust between the team and the congregation. Some congregations have a system to pray regularly for their leaders.

Develop Your Leaders

Churches often arbitrarily choose people for leadership. They rarely encourage potential leaders to go through a season of discernment, training, and development. Throughout the Bible, leaders developed other leaders by example and principle. Moses is a great biblical example of someone who thought he was not up to the task before him. But he had others to come around him, to lift his arms, to counsel him. The best example of a mentoring leader is Jesus. He spent three years mentoring and developing His apostles. Should we do any less in raising church leaders?

If this seems an overwhelming undertaking in your church's life, an S³ Intentional Interim Pastor can be a helper, advisor, and guide.

The Apostle Paul is another good example. He was not only a church planter, he was also an interim helper who returned to churches and identified and developed leaders. He offered correction and instruction. Titus provides yet another example of an interim pastor helper. Paul sent him to Crete to strengthen an established church which had been doing the work of evangelizing. In Titus 1:5, he commissioned Titus to "set things in order," employing the word *"ortho,"* which in Greek means to fix a broken bone. In developing leaders, Titus repaired as well as prepared workers for the harvest. In many respects, Titus was a church wellness expert. As are experienced and skilled S³ interim pastors.

Every church needs to straighten the crooked, get kinks out of the chain, and identify and develop leaders. Sometimes churches need a simple short-term fix. Other times a long-term intensive correction is required. Repair work is a regular part of church life, even today.

View the challenge of this transition as an opportunity to grow and develop. During this season, you can go deeper in prayer with God, be more connected with team members, learn new skills, and become more confident in your capability and contribution. Imagine this time between pastors as a semester in the school of leadership development. Leaders do not merely go through a pastoral transition. Instead, they grow through it!

Leadership Challenge: Many leadership teams meet monthly. We recommend that your leadership also meet about once per month for a time of relational and spiritual development. Read a book like *Spiritual Leadership* by Oswald Chambers or *The Measure of a Man* by Gene Getz. Reflect and comment on what you read. Slowly trust one another with self-disclosure. Ask for help where help is needed. Read a Psalm when you are together. Soak in God's Word. Pray together. Sometimes pray as a group and other times break up into triplets. Take time to share your testimony. As the relationships deepen, ask each person to respond to this statement: Talk about a sacred moment in your life. Go deeper with God and one another.

CALL TO ACTION

- Identify the leadership capacities and roles needed within your church to function with excellence and godliness.

- Describe the spiritual and emotional health and sense of unity and community within your leadership team and other ministry teams.

- Determine actions needed to improve the spiritual and emotional health and sense of unity and community of leaders in the church.

- Evaluate and enhance your church's processes for identifying, training, and developing leaders.

CALL TO PRAYER

- Pray for the leaders of your church. They will have special stress and be required to handle many roles during the interim between pastors.

- Pray that God would help your church discover new potential leaders and begin training and developing them during the time between pastors.

- Pray for the S[3] Intentional Interim Pastor your church has called or is calling to lead you during this interim between pastors.

Developing Leaders During the Pastoral Transition

THE PROBLEM

After several unpleasant pastor departures, a church in Virginia had multiple health issues. It lacked clarity of mission (why they exist) and vision (where they are going). Its organizational structure was dysfunctional, and it had no leadership development pipeline. While there were many church issues, the leadership issue was paramount. How does a seasoned, skilled, and strategic Interim Pastor strengthen an ineffective organizational structure and Leadership Team during such a transition?

For many years, an autocratic pastor led the church and failed to equip other leaders. Inattention to leadership development eventually ended in a disastrous church split. The congregation was unable to recognize the problem was more than a pastoral issue. It was a leadership structure that contributed to pastor burnout and tension between the pastor and other leaders.

The church attempted to resolve the defective autocratic pastor model by moving to a two-board structure: a spiritual and program board and a second board to oversee physical and financial issues. It birthed a two-headed monster. After five years, the church's leadership structure crashed once again.

Rather than jumping into another pastoral search, the church knew it was in trouble and decided to call on Interim Pastor Ministries (IPM). They wanted to fix their broken leadership structure, and they asked me to help them. The church resolved to walk through a process to identify underlying health issues and align with biblical principles before calling another pastor.

THE PROCESS

The first step in addressing the defective organizational structure was to gain congregational buy-in that a change was needed and get their affirmation of the process. No change will "take" without congregational approval. So, rather than working exclusively with Leadership, I had to rally the whole church family. I strategically taught and preached from biblical texts that focused on the nature and character of the church, how the body of Christ functions, as well as the qualifications and roles of overseeing boards. I led them through IPM's assessment process to help them discover the church's core health issues.

The IPM church health tool revealed, among other things, the weakness and ineffectual outcomes of the church's leadership structure and decision-making processes. The church recognized its need to align with biblical standards for Leadership and make necessary structural changes. I helped them develop a biblical framework and plan for ongoing leadership recruitment, development, and deployment.

THE PRODUCT

This pastoral transition resulted in a renewed congregation, a clear vision, a revised, biblically-based organizational structure, and a pipeline to multiply leaders. I discipled key leaders-in-training whom the members unanimously affirmed as the overseeing leadership board.

When the church called its new pastor, he stepped into a healthy church, prepared for future ministry effectiveness.

Ascend Through Prayer

Climb When You Are on Your Knees

Would your church commit to pray for the interim process and the next pastor for 100 days?

———

Who are the people passionate about the church's God-given future who will form prayer triplets as an exemplary prayer catalyst for the whole church?

———

If a significant prayer process is successful, what do you see as some of the outputs and impacts for your church's future?

———

I (Tom) first flew when I was 20 years old. I bought a ticket to fly to Georgia to see a former pastor and friend. I was scared. As the airplane started taxiing down the runway, I was holding my breath. My hands clenched the armrests. The aircraft picked up speed. What if it did not get enough speed to lift off? When will this thing lift off? As I prayed, the plane lifted. The pilot came through!

When your pastor leaves, your church loses its head pilot, but it must keep flying. This is a time of uncertainty and promise, filled with so much potential, promise, and peril.

You dare not navigate this season without promoting an atmosphere of prayer and discernment in your congregation. Prayer must precede and sustain a successful pastoral transition. Supplication precedes strengthening.

The best leaders lead on their knees. As they build godly dependence into every church decision, the airplane of faith lifts off, for we have a prayer-answering God.

Prayer is a full acknowledgment that our lives depend on God. Without Him, we can do nothing. Dependent prayer is knowing that we have not because we ask not.

Prayer is a sincere and reverent conversation with God. It is a heart-to-heart intimate exchange, such as you might have with a dear friend. No holds barred. No secrets. No hiding. Transparency is required for your conversation with God to reach the level of spiritual communication you desire.

Do not overcomplicate prayer. Don't worry so much about how to do it. Simply do it. The biggest issue with prayer is that Christians do not pray enough. "Pray more" is probably the shortest, simplest, and best counsel about prayer that we can give.

Prayer is as much about listening as it is speaking. Have you ever visited a friend, asked him how things were going, and listened to him talk nonstop for the next hour? You might have learned a lot about him, but what did he learn about you that might help and encourage him with his issues? He never gave you a chance to offer a suggestion, or provide him with many insights into yourself.

Prayer is like a child's conversation with their father. It is

———

Praying with purpose and intention will deepen your church's spiritual life because you have something definite to pray for that concerns every one of your members.

———

natural for a child to ask his father for the things he needs, and the father longs to pour his life into the child. But if the child simply lists her wants and then hurries off to play without listening for a response from her father, the child misses out on what she really wants: a relationship with her father.

God is not a vending machine. You do not put in prayer coins and push one or more buttons to see your answer clatter down the chute into your hand. The point of prayer is a relationship, and that relationship is not just between you and the One to whom you pray. When God's people pray together, they build relationships. When they listen to the heart cries of their fellow congregants they draw closer.

The season between pastors is a time for your church to enter into an intentional season of prayer. You need to develop a strategy for ongoing, meaningful, discerning, encouraging prayer. Praying with purpose and intention will deepen your church's spiritual life because you have something definite to pray for that concerns every one of your members. There is no time in your church's life when you need to be closer to the Lord than when you are in pastoral transition.

You may feel paralyzed, thinking you have no leader to take you to a deeply spiritual place. Remember, you are God's church, his holy people. You have direct access to God the Father. Your Father. You do not need a high priest or intermediary to approach God. When your church is without a pastor, it is no time to put your spiritual access card on the shelf. This is when you need to go deeper into prayer and pound ceaselessly on the door.

In Luke 18, Jesus tells the story about the judge who cared nothing about what others thought of him, or whether his judgments were right or wrong. But a widow confronts him demanding justice so persistently that the judge finally gives it to her.

You are pleading with God to prepare the church for its future and, in time, reveal His choice for your next pastor. And beyond this specific request, your congregation is seeking to go deeper with God to gain the wisdom to foster unity, and discover your identify. You are asking God to reveal His vision for the church. Overall, you are pleading with God to become a healthy church that will attract a healthy pastor.

If you are building a church on human ingenuity, strength, and ideas, you will fail. If there is ever a time to hear from the Lord, it is when a church is in pastoral transition.

100 Days of Discernment
Using Dialogue and Prayer Triplets

In my (Tom's) ninth intentional interim ministry, I discovered an extraordinary church prayer strategy that ignites the fire of spiritual discernment and development. It's called 100 Days of Discernment using Dialogue and Prayer Triplets. I

(George) crafted this spiritual process. My book entitled *Pursuing the Full Kingdom Potential of Your Congregation* (Chalice Press, 2005) fully explains this prayer strategy. You can also find it at *www.BullardJournal.org.*

The church's journey during a pastoral transition begins with a season of conversation and prayerful meditation. The focus is a new depth of relationship with one another and God. During a transition, a leap forward requires a foundation of relational prayer.

Here's how it works. Interested members and attendees form dialogue and prayer triplets. While you should encourage participation, do not make it a requirement, or pressure people to participate. Only those whose heart yearns to discern God's will for your church should join the effort. The higher the percentage of your congregation who do this together, the greater the church-wide impact.

I (Tom) used George's process to develop our 100-day prayer season for a church in transition where I was interim pastor. This church had an attendance of 425, and 225 signed up to pray in triplets. Our faith and anticipation grew as we called out to our Heavenly Father for His way and will for our church. As the Lord revealed to us His will, we experienced relational and spiritual revival. The 100-day process had a tremendous impact on us.

While I (Tom) have only implemented this prayer strategy in one church, George has facilitated it in hundreds of churches directly, and thousands more through his published process. Many churches report that this is the most significant spiritual experience they have had with their church family.

Are you ready? Is there a strong desire in the congregation to be captivated by God's empowering vision for the next stage? Are you willing to set aside some programs to allow time and space for the dialogue and prayer process? This spiritual journey is too essential to layer it on top of everything else the congregation is doing. Call time out and suspend some programs so the whole church has opportunity to participate.

The Dialogue and Prayer Triplet Process

The 100 Days of Discernment Using Dialogue and Prayer Triplets has three phases: Initiation, Implementation, and Impact. While the process is gradual it may have the immediate effect of uniting the church around a common purpose and to seek God's will. Praying together regularly will build a spirit of unity that will bless your church far into the future.

Initiation: The first phase is to identify, gather, and orient the dialogue and prayer triplets through two recruitment rounds. First, the organizers invite the People of Pastoral Leadership, the People of Passion, and the People of Position in your church to form dialogue and prayer triplets. The first numerical goal is for at least 21% of adult Sunday attendees to engage in dialogue and prayer triplets.

Second, the entire active congregation is invited to form dialogue and prayer triplets among themselves, with as many as possible participating.

People of Pastoral Leadership are the ordained ministers

on a church staff and other key staff program leaders. Typically, this group represents one percent or so of the average weekly worship attendance.

People of Passion represent approximately the next six percent of active attendees. It is self-evident that these people have a positive spiritual passion for the church's future. Passion is not a formal role or elected office in a church. These people have passion whether or not they are on staff. While some will hold recognized positions, they are recognized more by their passion than position.

People of Position are approximately the next 14 percent of active attendees. They are people with a formal role, and include elected officers, or key volunteers in a church whom were not previously identified as People of Passion.

In round one, these three groups form triplets. A minister, staff person, or person of passion leads each triplet. People of Position make up the other two participants in a triplet. For this to work, the first round's guidelines must be faithfully followed and completed before moving to round two.

It is important that the triplets not include people who are best friends. As much as the church's size and diversity will allow, the three people in a triplet need to be people who would benefit by getting to know one another better. This creates greater understanding, unity, and inclusiveness in the church.

Round two is an open invitation for everyone else in the church to sign up to be in a triplet. They can even identify the other two people with whom they want to dialogue and pray. Strive for diversity in these triplets in terms of age, gender,

————

Are you willing to set aside some programs to allow time and space for the dialogue and prayer process?

————

ethnicity, and length of time people have been attending the church. While family prayer is always a blessing and highly encouraged, for this process, you do not want any triplet to be composed of husband, wife, other relatives, or close friends. Achieving this diversity can be a challenge in smaller membership congregations.

Once the organizers identify the dialogue and prayer triplet participants, gather the participants for a launch event where they will be commissioned and provided with an orientation to the process. It is essential for the participants to understand they are being commissioned into a spiritual process to begin clarifying the mission of God for the church, to dialogue about the church's vision for the next seven years, and to discern God's will for their future. They also want to define the characteristics needed in their next pastor.

Develop and issue a manual that describes the dialogue and prayer process for the triplets' ten sessions over the next 100 days. *www.BullardJournal.org* has a sample manual available. The triplets can meet for about 30 minutes during the commissioning and orientation meeting to make logistical preparations for when and where they will assemble as a triplet.

Implementation: The second phase is the actual 100 days of discernment during which the triplets meet ten times according to the plan they developed during the commissioning and orientation. Here's a simple way to remember their commitment to the triplet: meet ten times for up to 100 minutes each time over the next 100 days. The first gathering or two will likely be brief as members learn to grow into the freedom and blessing of such a dialogue and prayer time. As participants become more familiar with each other, their sessions will grow longer as they dive deeper into dialogue and prayer.

The triplets meet as a large group for a mid-discernment dialogue and prayer time at around day 50 of the 100 days.

This session will begin with a large group activity, followed by a small group activity for six to nine people, and ends as a large group challenge.

During the opening session, a few triplet participants speak to the whole group about their experience, addressing the following questions: What's going well for you? What challenges do you face when it comes to gathering and spending quality time? What does the process mean, and how important is it to you? What were some of your first impressions?

Triplet participants then gather in groups of six to nine to address similar questions, and perhaps some of these: How is it going for your triplet? Are you meeting regularly? If not, can others suggest methods of meeting that are working for them? What do they discern God is inspiring in them through their triplet? What are they hearing from the Lord as they pray and discern God's will for the church? How have they grown closer to each other? What benefits are accruing to the church through this special time? Do you have any questions you want to pose to the larger group?

The encouraging reports from other groups will inspire some triplets who have not achieved their target of regular gatherings. The second half of the time of discernment will be even richer.

Any questions that emerged from the small group discussion should be addressed during the closing large group session. A report page in the sample manual asks each triplet to create and list five to seven observations, discernments or calls to action for the church from their 100 days together. Finally, the interim pastor or another church leader should give the congregation a spiritual challenge to promote their commitment to the process and focus on the church's success thus far.

The organizers invite the entire church to a celebration session at the end of the 100 days. Participants share their observations, compiled insights, discernments, and calls to action. The church's leadership team will receive this work for review and appropriate action. There will also be an opportunity for some triplet participants to give a testimony of their experience. The session concludes with a time of prayer and additional spiritual challenge.

Impact: In the third phase the leadership team develops a report and any appropriate recommendations for action. Based on the insights gained during the 100 days, the church can plan concrete steps for incremental, innovative actions. Just think of the excitement a new pastor will have coming into a church that has gone through this intentional, specific period of discernment and spiritual growth.

In addition to the insights they achieve, you will find a new depth of relationships and an atmosphere of prayer within the congregation. You will see increased spiritual depth and an ongoing practice of prayer in the lives of many participants. Many churches report that the end of the 100 days process they were different. They had changed.

The discernment period often brings a new spiritual and strategic energy to the congregation which helps them make the changes required to move forward under God's leadership, and improve the quality and effectiveness of the church's ministry.

In the church referenced earlier, where Tom used the 100 days process, the church realized that its 83-year-old governance model was not working. Their last pastor had tried to update the governance style years before, but opposition to change stopped progress in its tracks. After the discernment period and meetings with strategic staff, leaders, and members, the church formulated and unanimously approved a new governance model.

Reflecting on this, Tom says, "God is the One who prepared the hearts and revealed His will. He can do the same thing for your church."

Triplets in Action

I (George) arrived early one Wednesday afternoon at the church where I served as interim pastor. I needed to finish preparations for the mid-week Bible study that evening.

The secretary shared with me that Lisa was waiting to see

me in the library. I was not surprised that Lisa wanted to see me. She was one of our most faithful library volunteers and often had questions. But her question surprised me. Lisa was one of more than a dozen people in this smaller membership congregation who had signed up to lead a prayer triplet.

The prayer triplets were meeting that week for the first time. Lisa was still putting her triplet together, and had one person to add. She wanted to ask me about someone who might fill the spot. Lisa reported that on Tuesday morning, during her devotional time, she began to feel that God wanted the third person in her triplet to be a homebound person. She wanted to know if this was acceptable and did not break the rules.

This homebound person, Sarah, had not been able to attend church for worship for more than four years due to her declining physical health. Yet, her mind was very active. She kept up with the church, prayed for the church, and every month faithfully mailed in her offering. I was thrilled. This homebound person should absolutely engage in a prayer triplet. I was so sure that I asked Lisa if I could announce it that night at the mid-week Bible study. Lisa asked Sarah, who said yes. She was ecstatic to be a part of the project. I reported Sarah's participation later that evening.

After the Bible study, Elizabeth approached me, as she did every Wednesday night. Elizabeth was chairperson of the pastoral search team, and always had a list of questions for me. Tonight, however, something was different. Elizabeth was shaking as she approached me. When I asked her what was wrong, she said it had to do with my announcement about Lisa's prayer triplet.

She explained that her triplet had met for the first time on Monday. They talked about how the church needed to be more inclusive of the homebound people in their congregation. The next morning, Lisa felt led to invite a homebound person to be part of her triplet! "Wow," she said, almost breathlessly. "This works."

That Sunday morning, I asked Elizabeth and Lisa to tell their story during worship. In subsequent Sunday morning services, a different person spoke each week about what God was doing in and through their triplet.

Pray Everywhere and at All Times

Saturate church life with prayer. Pray at home, under the tree, in the car, at bedtime. Pray morning, noon, and night. Always pray everywhere and without ceasing.

Find the prayer warriors in your congregation. Ask them to pray that the church mount up with wings like eagles—to ascend toward God's greatness and grace. Pray that the Lord will bless your church and open the heavens and shower your church with health, fruit, and vitality.

Perhaps you will establish an intercessory prayer team. Have this team form an email distribution to invite people to pray and include a list of prayer requests. Would your people respond to prayer walks, bathing the church facility and property, and the neighborhood in prayer? The 100 Days of Discernment is a time to teach prayer on prayer and the

—————

Developing a holy dependence on God will unify your congregation as you work through the challenges. You will emerge from your transition and into your new vision, whole and healthy.

—————

experience of group prayer.

Consider opening the doors to the worship center on a particular day and time and invite anyone to come and pray. Encourage Bible study or Sunday school classes and other small groups to attend and pray as a group.

In many seminary preaching classes toward the end of the semester, every student must give a sermon. Because there are so many students, presentation time is limited. It is not uncommon for the preaching student to race through the scripture reference to get to what he thinks is the heart of the text.

After a few such presentations in his preaching class, Professor Joel Gregory stopped the proceedings. He reminded the students that the most important words of their sermon were the scripture text on which they preached.

Give your prayer time that kind of emphasis. Do not mumble a few trite phrases, capped by a resounding "in Jesus' name" and feel that you have communicated with the God of the universe. Your prayers do not inform God of anything He does not already know. Your prayers are an opportunity to hear from God what you do not know.

Devote time to prayer. Do not relegate prayer to an item that sanctifies the agenda. Take time to listen. As you grow in trust, lead your fellow church members to be transparent, even vulnerable in their prayers.

The congregation that I (Tom) led during the interim embraced the reality that we are a spiritual community, not a social club. Honest, earnest prayer is unique to a spiritual community. I am not talking about the nods to "In God We Trust" kinds of prayers that open civic and government meetings. A spiritual community is in communion with God. Prayer is the heart of the community. Without it, we are simply a social club.

As the church prayed they were led by God's Spirit to make changes. They reorganized their church governance, and adopted a profound mission statement that, in six words, summarized the Great Commission—*Share Christ, Build Believers, Serve Others.* A visioning process ran concurrently with the prayer time, and a spirit of love and unity prevailed as they made difficult decisions.

They possessed a sense of awareness of God's activity in their lives and the church. People from other congregations, who saw how God's spirit was moving our church, visited me to ask about our prayer ministry and how they could see similar results.

For a church in transition between pastors, prayer is not optional. Without prayer, you are simply making cultural, procedural, and organizational decisions. Prayer heightens awareness of your dependence on God for spiritual leadership open to being led, and able to discern next steps.

Unfortunately, congregations often spend more time

preaching about prayer than praying. An intentional prayer effort, with prayer triplets within congregational members, meeting for ten times, for 100 minutes, over 100 days will infuse your church body with a deep awareness of God, an openness to God's leading, healing of hurts, and a melding of hearts across generations.

———

During this interim period, you are asking God to show favor to your church. You are imploring him to lead and guide you, to replace your desires with His desires for the church, to meld your hearts into His.

———

It will fill your congregation with an overwhelming sense of rejoicing, connectedness to one another and God, and a refreshing openness to change so that you are ready to embrace something new.

In the absence of this season of intentional, community prayer, church discussions are more likely to devolve into competitive struggles: Who among us is right? Who wins and who loses?

Developing a holy dependence on God will unify your congregation as you work through the challenges. You will emerge from your transition and into your new vision, whole and healthy. You will know what God wants because your hearts have been humbled, cracked open like a walnut under a truck tire and willing to say to God, "Yes, tell us! Show us! We will follow."

Paul tells us in I Thessalonians to *pray without ceasing.* Jesus commands us to pray. James says we do not have what we want and need because we do not ask God for it.

When we talk of a prayer strategy or a prayer emphasis, we are not talking about a single prayer led by the preacher. We are talking about a movement of Spirit-led prayer that infuses your congregation like two teaspoons of red powder from a packet that can transform a glass of water into a fruit drink.

If you do not have an intentional prayer strategy, the interim period is an excellent time to start. Involve everyone who wants to participate. Enlist a praying volunteer to coordinate requests. Call upon the living God to break the crust that encases your heart, breathe new life into you, arresting the work of the enemy, and freeing your Spirit to be light in a dark world.

Teach the children in your church to pray in a meaningful way. On the other end of the age spectrum, your senior adults have a different perspective from which to pray. All who love the church are conversing with God on its behalf.

Intentional prayer is so essential that one large denomination has an office designated solely to prayer. Their minister's role is to lead and teach prayer in churches, offer prayer guides and prompts, and hold prayer retreats.

Earnest Prayer

Earnest prayer empties us of self, and fills us with the Lord. We listen to and discern His will and way for the Church.

Earnest prayer begins with worshipping and adoring the greatness of God. We center our attention and affection on

Him. As we lay our souls bare before Him, repent, and ask His forgiveness, He cleanses us from all sin. In prayer, we are vulnerable to God and to each other. Prayer triplets are so valuable because they require we trust one another. People who meet together in small groups regularly to dialogue and pray build that trust.

It is still right and proper to pray for your needs. Voicing them to God does not inform Him of your needs. God knows them thoroughly before you utter them. Hearing your own voice as you converse with God, and lay your needs at His feet, helps you to acknowledge your trust, and shed your burdens and cares.

Pray for other people's needs. Voicing the pains, needs, and wants of others helps make you aware of the larger world and decreases your self-focus. Be sure to always praise and thank God for His blessings in your life.

During this interim period, you are asking God to show favor to your church. You are imploring him to lead and guide you, to replace your desires with His desires for the church, to meld your hearts into His. Listen for what God is saying to your church, to you. God may be speaking conviction as well as assurance.

As God shows your church corrective actions, you must act now. By responding to His revelations, you are becoming the right kind of church that can call the right kind of pastor to lead you.

In Revelation, God had a specific message for each of the seven churches. What is God's message to your church? If

God wrote the eighth letter to your church, what would He commend, warn, rebuke, and what directives would he give you and your church?

Sometimes God will reveal some low-hanging fruit, simple, quick, straightforward actions you can take. Other times, he will show a more profound and deeper change he wants to bring to the congregation. Perhaps, he will reach down and open everyone's eyes to relational discord and his desire to bring unity. When God speaks, we must act. To not act is to disobey. Keep in mind, however, some steps God asks you to take are so large that you need to wait until a new pastor has gotten his feet on the ground, and is ready to take those steps with you.

One Last Thought

This chapter is not a manual on prayer. We are trying to highlight the importance of establishing a spiritual growth strategy and discernment during this critical interim period. Churches that already have such a plan are well-positioned to respond in faith and not panic, no matter what occurs. Such an effort will sustain and move your congregation into the future God has for you.

Above all, pray without ceasing.

CALL TO ACTION

- Organize the 100 Days of Prayer using dialogue and prayer triplets.

- Identify the people in your congregation who are passionate about the church and its future. Typically, you are looking for a number that is around seven percent of the average number of adults present on a typical Sunday.

- Determine the goals for the 100 Days process. What will be the output and impact of this process?

CALL TO PRAYER

- Pray that the people who ought to be involved in a dialogue and prayer triplet will come forward and participate.

- Pray for your S[3] Intentional Interim Pastor and his leadership of the church.

- Pray for the church leadership team and other leadership groups as they seek to guide the church's steps during the transition between pastors.

- Pray that the new people who visit your church during the transition might experience a church fellowship earnestly seeking God's leadership.

Intentional Prayer
Energizes the Church

THE REALITY

After more than 30 years, the church's beloved pastor retired. Members were at a loss emotionally, relationally, and spiritually, with little vision for their future. As the interim pastor, I asked church leaders two questions:

"How visible is prayer in your church?" and "Where do you see prayer taking place?" These questions, not surprisingly, were met with "deer in the headlights" responses:

- "Well, our pastor taught on prayer."
- "We believe in prayer."
- "We've read books on prayer."
- "We used to have an all-church prayer night."
- "Prayer is not very visible, but it must be happening. Right?"

Sadly, the answer to the last question is, "Probably not." There is a big difference between having some church members who pray and being a praying church. Both matter, but the biblical practice is a church praying together. I immediately focused on mobilizing, leading, demonstrating, and training others in prayer so that they could become prayer leaders in their setting.

I hoped that a few of these would continue to lead this prayer effort by the end of my interim when the new pastor came on board. And they did, to my great joy. They continue to grow in prayer, and the genesis for their deepening prayer life was the transition between lead pastors. Fueled by prayer, churches can leap and not lag during an interim period.

THE RESPONSE

My first steps at the church were to observe, listen, and discern: "to build walking paths where footprints already exist."

There's no reason to reinvent a wheel that's already rolling, but in this case there were no wheel, spokes, or hub.

I began with church leadership—staff, elders, deacons—to make prayer the priority, the first thing we do. It would no longer be absent in our gatherings or tucked in to signal the end of the meeting. We established a biblical foundation of prayer by focusing primarily on Jesus' teaching in Matthew 6:9-13, and the ongoing prayer practices of the early church, found in Acts.

I wanted leaders who understood prayer to be a biblical mandate, not just a new way of doing an old thing. Once I laid the biblical foundation through teaching and modeling, we were ready for the next step. By this time, I was meeting regularly on early Sunday mornings to pray with my ministry team.

I continued to raise the bar through a six-week sermon series on prayer, complemented by a compelling small group DVD series. We began to make prayer a priority in our church services and not just an add-on. We emphasized prayer from the platform, in small groups, and through directed prayer and testimonies, etc. We concluded this series by establishing a monthly Sunday evening prayer gathering.

THE RESULT

The new pastor arrived at a praying church where people longed for more of Jesus. Of course, some late adopters were not quite sure about this prayer movement, but many came aboard.

Such is the life of any interim pastor who determines his primary role is "the ministry of the Word and the ministry of prayer" (Acts 6:4). I continue to rejoice in how this church is continuing to make prayer its priority, following God in obedience as they hear His voice.

The best leaders and churches lead from their knees.

Bow down!

Action 5

Become a C³ Church
Soar into the Future

What are the Great Commission Mission, Enduring Core Values, and God's Empowering Vision for your church?

—

Are your leaders ignited by that vision?

—

How well do you reflect the characteristics of the very early Christian Church?

—

By now you know that I (Tom) fly a lot. When I am in my frugal mood, I fly Spirit Airlines. When I am feeling more expansive, I travel on one of the legacy carriers like Delta, United, American, or Southwest. My dream is to fly internationally one day on the number one rated airline in the world, Singapore Airlines.

What makes Singapore Airlines so divine? How about having an international culinary panel comprised of eight world-renowned chefs creating the onboard menus with items like seafood pasta with fresh shrimp, oysters, and salmon bites. Rather than training new flight attendants for the industry-standard two months, Singapore Airlines trains them for four months. It shows in the service they provide. They say you "fly like a king" on Singapore Airlines.

What distinguishes one airline from all the others? They

all have planes made primarily by Boeing or Airbus. Each gets people from point A to point B. Here is how I pick an airline. My criteria are good service, excellent safety record, generous comfort, lower prices, and they fly to my destination. When I find an airline that checks all the boxes, I buy a ticket and take off. It is all about which airline is a great fit for me.

The same is true for churches looking for a new lead pastor. If a church is going to take off and fly, it needs a pastor who is a great fit. We call this a P³ Lead Pastor. This is a pastor who is *passionate, proactive*, and *personable*.

P³ pastors are *passionate* about the Good News of Jesus Christ and know how to effectively preach and teach the gospel. They are *proactive* in their leadership style, gifted in casting vision, and aligning and leading the church to fulfill that vision. Finally, they are *personable*. They love their people and lead them with deep compassion. (See Action Seven for more details on a P³ Lead Pastor.)

A C³ Soaring Church

In preparation for your next lead pastor, your S³ Intentional Interim Pastor can help your church become a C³ Soaring Church whose life is characterized by D³ Intentionality. A C³ Soaring Church clearly understands that its prime directive is the *Great Commission* in the spirit of the *Great Commandment*. This is God's mission for the church. Church leaders have deep ownership of its enduring core values, and are captured by vision that comes from God and not the next pastor or the church members.

To conduct an effective pastoral search and call a P³ Lead Pastor, your church must have a firm grasp on three things:

1. Its prime directive from God, the Great Commission Mission.

2. Its Enduring Core Values.

3. God's Empowering Vision. Where is the church going in the next seven years? How is the church going to strategically align itself to God's vision using D³ Intentionality?

Action Five addresses the Great Commission Mission, the Enduring Core Values, and God's Empowering Vision. Action Six will address D³ Intentionality with strategic alignment. Action Seven will show that it is essential pastoral candidates be able to share their mission, values, and vision. You will want to call a P³ Lead Pastor whose identity matches your church's identity. For that to happen, both parties must clarify who they are through the articulation of their mission, values, and vision.

Your church undoubtedly already has a mission statement which expresses your primary identity as a New Testament church. The time between pastors is an excellent opportunity to examine, affirm, reclaim, or refine your identity. Does it incorporate a Great Commission Mission, a set of Enduring Values, and God's Empowering Vision?

Great Commission Mission

Mission answers the *"what"* question: What is the overall prime directive for the Christian Church which should be evident in each local church? The mission of a church is the same

---

The time between pastors is an excellent opportunity to examine, affirm, reclaim, or refine your identity.

---

for every church but may be expressed in different words.

The church's mission is the Great Commission in the spirit of the Great Commandment. In Matthew 28:18-20 we read, "Go, therefore and make disciples of all nations, baptizing them in the name of the Father, the Son, and the Holy Spirit, teaching them to observe all that I have commanded you. And behold, I am with you always, to the end of the age."

Mark 12:28-31 tells us about the Great Commandment:

One of the scribes came up and heard them arguing, and recognizing that He had answered them well, asked Him, "What commandment is the foremost of all?" Jesus answered, "The foremost is, 'Hear, Israel! The Lord is our God, the Lord is one; and you shall love the Lord your God with all your heart, and with all your soul, and with all your mind, and with all your strength.' The second is this: 'You shall love your neighbor as yourself.' There is no other commandment greater than these."

The mission question that arises from the Great Commandment is this: Are we sharing the Good News of Jesus, developing disciples, multiplying disciples, and continually engaging in actions of compassion? A New Testament church should always be in prayer about how it will embrace its role in the Great Commission in the spirit of the Great Commandment. How will it share Christ locally and globally?

If you have a mission statement that reflects these biblical directives, the prospective lead pastor will know at least in word and concept that you take the mission of God seriously. That will help him begin to make his own God-inspired decision about his possible future with your church.

Mission statements are akin to mottos or taglines in the overall communication of the identity of a church. However, a mission statement is transferable to any Great Commission church. It does not yet say how a specific church understands its spiritual and strategic direction, which can only come

————

Mission statements are akin to mottos or taglines in the overall communication of the identity of a church.

————

through God's Empowering Vision.

One church where I (Tom) served as an Intentional Interim Pastor crystallized their Matthew 28:18-20 mission statement in just six words—*Share Christ, Build Believers, and Serve Others*. This is a statement similar to one that can be experienced in the ministry of many churches.

The big question is, does your church have a mission statement? Is it time to evaluate, update, and reaffirm it? Or do you need to craft a new one?

Enduring Core Values

Values answer the "why" question: Why do we do what we do? What is our motivation? What forms the foundation of our spiritual life together? What is so important to us that it is not open to negotiation?

Highly regarded church consultant Aubrey Malphurs referenced values when he said, "You'll never do ministry that matters until you articulate what matters."

A look at the activity of the early Church in the book of Acts can help us form our values. Beginning in Acts Chapter 2, we learn how we might do church in a way that reflects how the earliest believers did it.

Acts 2:42-47 describes church life for those first believers and shows us their essential values: worship, instruction, fellowship, evangelism, and service.

- In **worship**, we recognize God's worthiness and holiness—His "otherness"—and humbly lay our souls prostrate before the Lord.

- **Instruction** teaches God's Word and truth in the Holy Spirit's power so that people's lives are changed. They become not just hearers but doers also.

- **Fellowship** is relational loving and caring for one another, meeting the body's needs, centered in Christ.

- **Evangelism** is sharing the gospel through the power of the Holy Spirit. We explain the path of salvation through word and witness, hoping that people respond in faith and find Christ as their God and Savior.

- **Service** utilizes our gifts, treasures, and talents to build up believers and to demonstrate the love of Christ to those far from Christ.

Are these universal values and actions evident in your church? The interim period is a great time to evaluate and adjust. Remember, every step you take to consider, affirm, or improve your church helps create a path that is more easily followed by your next lead pastor.

God's fingerprints are on every church, giving each unique passion, gifts, and people. Churches vary in distinct ways, with different traditions and perspectives on worship styles, governance models, and other distinctives. But some values—those exhibited by the very early Church—are universal.

We will say more about the values and practices of the very early Church later in Action Five.

God's Empowering Vision

Vision answers the directional "where" question. Where are we headed? Where is God pulling us? What do our spiritual eyes and strategic imagination see ahead of us?

A church between pastors needs to pursue and discern God's Empowering Vision before it can undertake a pastoral search. Ask yourselves, where is our church headed, and where will it be in seven years if God blesses us?

Be instructed by the pattern reflected in Leviticus 25:1-12. Six seasons of planting, cultivating, and harvesting are followed by a year of sabbatical. The time between pastors is like a year of sabbatical. During that year prayerful discernment about God's Empowering Vision for your church's next season should be a priority.

Discovering your vision is hard work. Some make it confusing. Many churches and their leaders have tried different visions and strategies, until they become frustrated and confused.

Many churches say to pastoral candidates, "Bring us a new vision." This is hardly ever a good approach. It is not wise to throw up your hands and ask your new pastor to bring you a

———

Vision is not a statement that is memorized.
It is a movement of God that is memorable.

———

vision. He may bring you a vision your church does not like or support. When a new pastor casts an unwelcome vision, it often leads to church conflict, a church split, or the firing of that new pastor. When your new pastor sets out on his own new journey, and few take the trip with him, you have trouble.

Asking a new pastor to bring vision indicates a major misunderstanding of how churches arrive at a vision. It must be their own, and they must pursue it. The pastor is often the key voice of vision, casting it in various ways. I (George) do not believe vision is a 15-word or less statement that is proclaimed by the pastor or crafted in a committee and presented to the church. Vision is not a statement that is memorized. It is a movement of God that is memorable. It must be discerned and owned by the body. (See *Captured by Vision: 101 Insights to Empower Your Congregation*. WestBow Press, 2017)

During the time between pastors the respected leaders of the church may be the ones helping the church discern its vision. When this approach works well, the church will call a P³ Lead Pastor who has the spiritual gifts, life skills and ministry style preferences that fit the vision.

Does casting a new vision limit your next pastor. Not in the least. A vision does not represent the full spiritual and strategic plan for a church involving goals and action plans. Your church may have a short-term strategy for 18 to 36 months, but when a new pastor arrives, he can help you look at a full seven years in ways that help leadership fulfill God's Empowering Vision for your church.

Leadership can communicate to candidates the church's preferred destination. This will help them see how you discern God's leadership, while giving him the opportunity to work with the leaders and congregation to discover a more long-range strategic journey. Again, it is another tool by which both parties can measure the likelihood that they are a good match.

What Is God's Empowering Vision?

Vision provides a clear, challenging, and ever-changing picture of God's full Kingdom potential for your church. Unlike a Great Commission Mission which can apply to every church, God's Empowering Vision is meant specifically for your church based on the community of people who form your church, and the context in which your church ministers.

Vision helps your church live into God's future. Your

church will be different. It will change as it follows God's vision over the next seven years. Often the vision that churches cast is internally focused. These churches change the least because this is a limiting approach focused on the gathered church.

More powerful visions focus on the Great Commission in the spirit of the Great Commandment. Applied to your church's context, this vision will transform your church with the unconditional love of God through Jesus Christ. How will your context be transformed as your church fulfills God's Empowering Vision?

Vision is a clear, challenging picture of the future, as you believe it can and must be, as imparted by God. Vision is the intersection of God's desire and mission and the local congregation's passion and giftedness within its context. At its core, vision is not where we want to see the church going, but where God wants it to go. It is God's vision for the full Kingdom potential of your church that you must discern and seek to fulfill.

When your church discovers and lives into God's vision, it begins to fulfill its potential.

President John F. Kennedy famously said, "Some people see things the way they are and ask, 'Why?'; I see things the way they could be and ask, 'Why not?'" Robert Greenleaf spoke of the power of vision when he wrote, "Nothing much happens without a dream, and for something great to happen, there must always be a great dream."

Crafting a Vision

Remember, vision is not a statement made by people. It is a movement of God that is memorable. It might be captured in a statement, but only after it is a movement.

Vision can start out as a story which can only be written in response to the following question: If our church lives into the call of God on us, describe what we will be like seven years from now. What will characterize us? What will we be doing?

Once the future story of missional ministry is clear, the congregation can back-cast and answer the question—Given the picture of what we will be seven years from now, how do we put into words what we want to do in the next seven years?

Vision Is in the Driver's Seat

After a lifetime of studying, consulting with, and leading congregations across the USA and Canada, if I (George) were to name the four primary elements of the modern church, they would be the following: Vision, Relationships, Programs, and Management. Every church has these elements in some measure. They must all work together in harmony for the church to fully thrive.

Imagine these four elements are passengers in a sports utility vehicle—a metaphor I regularly use. Where should each of them sit? Who should be driving? Who is backseat driving? Who is navigating? Is anyone along for the ride? Is the vehicle heading in the right direction? How would anyone know? (See my book, *Captured by Vision: 101 Insights to Empower Your Congregation.* WestBow Press, 2017.)

The pastor is not the sole source of your church's vision. Vision is the intersection of God's desires, the passion of the local congregation, and your community's needs.

Vision begins with knowing where the car is going. If you do not know where you are going, any road will do. A church on a mission knows where it is going as vision steers the SUV.

Don't take this metaphor too far by assuming one person represents the driver. The pastor is not the sole source of your church's vision. Vision is the intersection of God's desires, the passion of the local congregation, and your community's needs. A church needs a general sense of vision or direction before it can do a pastoral search.

Relationship rides shotgun, occupying the navigation seat next to the driver. The Great Commission in the spirit of the Great Commandment can only be fulfilled through relationships which grow and intensify during the journey. These include everyone's relationship to God (salvation and personal spiritual growth), to one another (serving and helping other believers grow in Christ), and to the world (witnessing to the lost in words and good works).

Programs are intended to support relationships. Programs are not the vision, the goal, or the navigator. They support. If programs become the goal or navigator—or the reason your church functions—it's only because the congregation has no vision.

I have often heard church leaders say it is so much harder

to kill a program that is not working than it is to start something new. Too many programs or having the wrong programs can weigh your church down for lack of volunteers, lack of measurable impact, or too big a drain on the budget.

Management is in the back seat behind vision. Management helps determine what direction the church should go, what programs it should fund, and what risks are taken. Giving prominence to management or programs over relationships will dim a church's vision.

How Did the Very Early Church Do It?

A body of believers cannot be a New Testament church unless they do what the very early Church did. The early Church lived out the Great Commission, even when they were not yet known as Christians (see Acts 11). New Testament church movements of God do the same.

In the upper room, the Holy Spirit filled the early Christians, comforting and transforming them. The apostles were released to act with conviction and courage, even in a hostile environment. Peter grew overnight from chump to champion, preaching Jesus with great vigor.

Early Christians comprised an uncommon church full of people with an extraordinary life together. We find in Acts 2:42-47 the values and characteristics that made them uncommon, against which you can compare your own church's identity as a New Testament church.

What are those characteristics? Before they were even known as Christians, early Jesus followers had (1) An

Uncommon Experience with God's Word, (2) An Uncommon Life of Fellowship, (3) An Uncommon Prayer Life, (4) An Uncommon Worship, (5) An Uncommon Expectation of the Miraculous, (6) An Uncommon Generosity, and (7) An Uncommon Witness.

An Uncommon Experience with God's Word: Before any written New Testament, the very early Church had the Living Word of God—Jesus the Christ. "And the Word became flesh and dwelt among us" (John 1:14). They also had the voice of God. "My sheep hear My voice, and I know them, and they follow Me" (John 10:27). They had the writings that form much of the Old Testament and the habit of memorizing these scrolls.

The most uncommon and extraordinary expression of God's word available to the very early Church were the Apostles' testimonies and teachings. The apostles spent three years experiencing the Living Word of God and His relationship with His Father. This powerful reality of Jesus' bodily presence helped people to demythologize what it is like to relate to God the Father. It showed them in real time the real-life experiences of the Living Word of God.

Today, we have even more—we have the complete word of God, which is, of course, the 66 books that make up the Bible. We read, study, and live its teachings. Through the Holy Spirit Jesus meets us in a profound personal way as read the Word. It feeds our souls and directs our paths as we walk in the way of Jesus .

Do your people have a deep personal relationship and

experience with Christ that fires them up? Does their spiritual vitality whet others' appetite and motivate them to also know, love, serve Christ, and winsomely attract others to Him?

An Uncommon Life of Fellowship: The very early Church had an extraordinary fellowship that cannot be translated or transliterated into any one word. The Greek word "koinonia," often translated "common," richly characterizes the term "fellowship." They had all things in common and enjoyed daily experiences of fellowship with one another.

Many church buildings have a room they call the fellowship hall, typically a place for food, fun, and fellowship. This perspective trivializes the concept of "fellowship" or "koinonia" present in the very early Church in many ways.

Biblical fellowship is sharing in a deep relationship with God, one another, and God's world. We are in accord with God and one another when we gather for worship, Bible study, discipleship development, ministry, food, and fun.

We are in fellowship with the people of God's world when we scatter into our community for work, play, shopping, education, sports, events, and so many other life activities. At our best, we represent a holy presence when we interact with people in a manner that illuminates the unconditional love of God.

As you consider how closely your Church reflects the early New Testament church, how would you evaluate your fellowship?

An Uncommon Prayer Life: The committed people of the

early Church continually devoted themselves to prayer in community with one another. Their group prayer united them. They demonstrated the truth that people who remember each other in prayer can survive differences which otherwise might divide them.

Today, people of an uncommon prayer life not only pray for family, friends, co-workers, and their church. They also pray by name for people who do not know Jesus Christ as their personal Lord and Savior. Their prayers are not restricted to personal issues, such as their well being, the difficulties they face, but encompass opportunities to spread the gospel of Jesus Christ and challenges to this work.

Do your group prayer times resemble more of an "organ recital" in which you pray more for hearts and lungs than for the Holy Spirit to draw others to himself?

An Uncommon Worship: Blending the first three uncommon characteristics of the very early Church results in uncommon worship full of awe, reverence, wonder, amazement, and spiritual esteem for all God has done, is doing, and will do.

The very early Church longed to worship. They rejoiced in worship. They did not merely "endure a worship service." They felt like their day—and how much more their week—was incomplete unless it involved worship and fellowship with other believers.

Indeed, it is not easy to sustain this intensity of worship day after day, week after week, and month after month unless Christians are captivated anew in each worship experience.

As we experience the wonder and majesty of our triune God, we encounter God's presence and enjoy fellowship with Him.

Our busyness, everyday habits, distractions, and the complacency that creeps into life can interrupt worship. When we prioritize our public and private worship, when we bow before God and praise His name, we experience the true worship of the Father, Son, and Holy Spirit.

How serious is your church about designing, planning, encouraging, praying for, and conducting worship experiences in fellowship with each other that will have your people yearning for more?

An Uncommon Expectation of the Miraculous: Through the Apostles, the very early Church experienced miraculous wonders and signs. Their life was anything but ordinary or routine. Life was extraordinary. They had just experienced the miraculous resurrection of Jesus. They lived in expectation of experiencing the supernatural through physical, psychological, and spiritual healings.

If we are to be like the believers in the very early Church, we will expect the miraculous, pray for the supernatural, and look for the extraordinary to happen. It is uncommon and unusual to expect the appearance of what to others seems impossible. It means setting goals that are not contingent on or limited by earthly success or prosperity. It requires our full surrender to the will of God and God's outpouring of answered prayer.

Expecting the miraculous involves thinking, praying, and acting on this question: What seems impossible today that if it could happen according to the will of God, would transform our ability to serve in God's Kingdom?

Are any such prayers being lifted in your congregation?

An Uncommon Generosity: Acts 2:45 says, "And they began selling their property and possessions and were sharing them with all as anyone might have a need." In other words, the very early Church gave generously to others, especially their brothers and sisters in Christ.

The very early Church likely expected Jesus to return soon, so they figured their shared resources would be enough until then. Obviously, Jesus has not returned (as of this writing), but I would suggest we ought to look at the gospels for a pattern of uncommon generosity,

In Matthew 19:21, Jesus suggests to the rich young ruler that he sell his possessions and give to the poor. In Matthew 6:24, as part of the Sermon of the Mount, Jesus said it is impossible to serve both wealth and God.

Jesus suggested to his disciples, as recorded in Luke 12:33, that they sell their possessions and give to the poor. Many other biblical passages refer to shedding possessions and caring for others. The very early Church was following the instruction of Jesus to be uncommonly generous.

Does your congregation operate from an attitude of generosity, or of scarcity? Do you examine the budget receipts before earnestly praying for opportunity? What portion of your personal revenues funds your Church?

An Uncommon Witness: The very early Church was both gathered and scattered. Jesus' followers were active and faithful witnesses of their experience. They saw a constant harvest brought to them by the Lord, who added to their number daily.

The modern Church must be intentional about its role as both a gathered and a scattered church. It is hard to be a witness if you are not reaching out to non-Christian people, going to places where you encounter and interact with them in a non-confrontational manner. How do you witness to non-Christians if you do not invite them into your home or church?

The very early Church scattered to find, engage, embrace, and win friends and neighbors to believe in and follow Christ: "And the word of God kept on spreading, and the number of the disciples continued to increase greatly" (Acts 6:7).

What is the witness of your church? Is it a beacon of light, love, ministry, and service in your community? Or is it a private weekly gathering of people careful not to sully their reputations by mixing with the unclean?

Consider these seven characteristics of an uncommon church as you evaluate how you reflect the New Testament church during this interim period.

CALL TO ACTION

- Reaffirm or discern and craft anew the mission, core values, and vision for your church.

- If God's Empowering Vision is not already the driving force in your church, focus on getting vision in the driver's seat of your church's journey.

- Study the characteristics of the very early church and seek to reflect them in the life and ministry of your church.

CALL TO PRAYER

- Pray for your church and its leaders as you engage in a process of reaffirming or drafting anew your mission, core values, and vision.

- Pray for God's leadership to discern God's will for the future of the church.

- Pray for the person God is already preparing to be the pastor of your church.

- Pray that as a C³ Soaring Church you may transform the context you serve with the unconditional love of God.

From a Church on the Ropes
to a Congregation Full of Hope

THE CIRCUMSTANCES

The church on the ropes was a group of Christ-followers whose church had lost its soul. The long-serving senior pastor was at odds with staff and elders. The staff team worked behind his back. Elders couldn't work together, so the congregation established a separate committee to do their work. The buildings needed repairs. I asked for their vision and mission statements. They didn't have a vision statement, but they did produce four conflicting mission statements. The church was barely surviving.

After the pastor finally left in a cloud of ill will, the church hired, then fired, two consultants when it didn't like their assessments and recommendations. In desperation, they called Interim Pastor Ministries, and I was assigned this reclamation project.

THE COURSE OF ACTION

My first three months consisted of one-on-one meetings with former and current staff, elders, and congregants. I grieved over their stories of how individuals called to serve got so out of sorts with each other that they divided into antagonistic groups. After many meetings, I composed a simple survey for all former and current staff, elders, and second-level leaders (i.e., small group leaders and ministry team leaders) to give me a fuller picture of the climate.

The survey showed that corporate and personal repentance was needed. Core values, mission, vision, and philosophy of ministry needed retooling. And some needed to be created. The church was isolated and needed to be connected with the lost and other like-minded churches. The elders and interim pastor came up with a job description that clearly defined the role of the Lead Pastor, staff, and elders.

Then, for the first time, the church held a Solemn Assembly. Members humbled themselves before God, confessing corporate sins. I challenged those carrying offenses to surrender their grievances to Jesus. Practicing Matthew 18, they went to those with whom they had unresolved differences to say, *"I'm sorry, will you forgive me?"* What followed was a time of great worship and praise, concluding with prayers of anticipation for the future, communion, and signing a covenant of personal and corporate renewal.

From this renewal, there arose a passion for reaching the community in creative ways. Staff initiated an outreach event called *"Christmas for the City"* and rented an ice-skating rink to offer as a gift to the community. We raised money to surround the rink, with Christmas activities and refreshments for the children. Those gifted in carpentry built booths where people prayed and received Christ. In seven days, 10,000 people came through the village, and our church exploded with a joy that could not be contained.

The church's momentum during the interim helped launch a capital campaign to upgrade the ministries and facilities.

THE CONSEQUENCES

It's been several years since the interim process finished. The "Church of Hope," once the "Church on the Ropes," is flourishing. Among their significant steps of progress:

- There is ongoing elder and staff training where the best practices of leadership are taught.
- To increase communication, and exert leadership, the elders publish monthly *Elder Endnotes*, in which they express the church's heart for missions and affirm its identity in Christ. It also allows the elders to reinforce the governing structure by vision casting glimpses of the future.
- New core values, mission, vision, and philosophy of ministry statements have been embraced and enhanced through various communications.
- We began communicating weekly with the congregation during the interim through an outline letter, *First Baptist*

Focus, with upgraded video, vision moments and electronic sign-ups. This communication letter continues.

- With new funds supplied by growth, the children's building was remodeled into a kid-friendly Kid's JAM (*Jesus and me*) facility and upgraded sanctuary video/sound systems.
- The church adopted a modified church governance model that delineated the elders, pastor, and staff's roles, relationships, and responsibilities.
- An annual *Global Focus* month instills the vision of a Great Commission church reaching the globe. We host and interview missionaries, show videos of their work, have live chats and place a strong focus on mission giving.
- In the first two and one-half years after the new pastor's arrival, the congregation grew by 32.6 percent and baptized 54.
- Fifty-six percent of the congregation served in a church or community ministry.
- And best of all, 117 people have made commitments to Christ.

Soar with
D³ Intentionality

Align Your Ministry with God's Empowering Vision

How well do your current processes, programs, and ministries (PPMs) align with God's Empowering Vision?

———

How do they intentionally support disciplemaking, developing leaders, and dynamic innovative execution?

———

How will you measure the intentionality, significance, and impact of your disciplemaking, developing leaders, and dynamic innovative execution?

———

Airplanes get you to your destination. At times they have to fly around bad weather, alter their course due to congestion in the flight patterns, or circle an airport waiting for a landing window to open. Frequent flyers such as the two of us (Tom and George) are periodically on flights that are running late. The pilot informs the passengers that flight controllers have granted the airplane a more direct flight path so that we can make up some lost time. In any case, the pilot's focus is always on the destination.

The same should be true in your church. The processes, programs, and ministries (PPMs) of your church should always be focused on your destination. Yet, just like with the flight of an airplane, a church experiences delays and detours. Members come and go. Staff come and go. And pastors come and go. Even pandemics happen. Often, God opens new doors we had not anticipated and the church moves more directly towards its destination.

The destination is the fulfillment of God's Empowering Vision. It will help your church journey in the direction of your full Kingdom potential. To do this you will need D³ Intentionality that focuses on *disciplemaking, developing leaders*, and *dynamic innovative execution*. Despite their good intentions, too many churches seem to have a disconnect between God's Empowering Vision and their PPMs. As a result, they are in flight, but headed to the wrong destination.

I (George) once coached a church which had been through a process similar to a C³ Soaring Church process, but within a year realized they were not making progress. They had a clear vision. It appeared to be deeply owned throughout the church. They were willing to engage in actions they thought would fulfill their vision, but no progress was being made.

To engage their situation, I first gained an understanding of their mission, core values, and vision. I learned about their context. Then I asked them to share the PPMs they were using to fulfill their vision. As they shared, I recognized these as older, traditional programs that did not fit their new vision.

I interrupted the conversation and made my observation. I asked them to share with me the new PPMs they were developing to fulfill God's Empowering Vision. They told me the

PPMs they had already shared with me were the ones they were using to fulfill God's Empowering Vision. They liked those PPMs and thought they would just do them with a new sense of energy and urgency, with the vision in mind.

Regretfully, I told them that would not work. They needed to develop new approaches using new methods focused on new people with newly developed leaders. They went away sad because they wanted a new vision, but they did not want to change their church in order to fulfill the vision. They had no plans to soar with D^3 Intentionality.

Evaluate Your Current Processes, Programs, and Ministries

Twentieth-century humorist Will Rogers said something like this, *"I'm tired of my taxes paying to build roads that will be worn out by Baptists going to meetings."* If weary churchmen sing any chorus in common, it is the demands of too many meetings.

It is easier to start a new program than to kill an existing, non-effective program. There are too many oxen to be gored, too many sensitive souls, and too many funerals for dead programs to plan.

Programs should never drive your church mission. Vision is the driver. Relationships—with God, one another, and the lost—are the navigator. How do you take advantage of this opportune time between pastors to look seriously at your PPMs, to give the new pastor an uncluttered path to chart his course?

Consider this: Are you conducting processes, programs,

and ministries only because certain members of your church love them? Leading these programs is how they define their week or their month. Do they derive their Christian identity from these programs?

Or are the PPMs loved by the people you are trying to reach? Ask yourself, who is the client? The customer? To

---

Programs should never drive your church mission. Vision is the driver. Relationships—with God, one another, and the lost—are the navigator.

---

whom has God sent us? God has not sent us to serve ourselves. More importantly, is the event value for itself, or is its real treasure the follow-up process that connects people to your church, each other, and the Kingdom?

If your church makes it to this point in the Soaring Between Pastors Framework introduced at the beginning of this book, the hope would be that you would embrace a new or renewed set of PPMs. You don't necessarily need to stop doing all of what you are doing, but you do need to evaluate your PPMs in light of your new understanding and commitment to God's Empowering Vision. Begin by evaluating your PPMs as to their potential effectiveness in helping you fulfill God's vision. Your S³ Intentional Interim Pastor can lead you through this process.

Your most impactful processes, programs, and ministries (PPMs) are those aligned with the fulfillment of God's vision, God's full Kingdom potential for your church. From the beginning of the evaluation, you must accept that some PPMs will need to be eliminated, some renewed in a different form, and some new ones will need to be launched.

Our experience shows that some people who agree that certain PPMs need to be modified or eliminated will challenge any attempts to change or stop PPMs for which they feel deep ownership. Other PPMs need to be changed or stopped, not theirs.

Leaders need courage and wisdom to deal with those suffering such loss. I (George) have taught for three decades that the perceived benefits of change must be at least twice as great as the perceived loss from the change. That is why you must dialogue and transition people's heart, soul, mind, and strength before you can change things.

Avoid simply adding the PPMs that focus on the fulfillment of your vision to what you are already doing. You must first change or eliminate some PPMs. Busyness will not help your church soar into the future, and old PPMs will simply interfere with the new ones.

It is counterintuitive but, you can accomplish more by doing less. It is better to do a few things exceptionally well, rather than doing many things with mediocrity as Thom Rainer and Eric Geiger's book *Simple Church* points out. Too many churches confuse activity with effectiveness. Here is the point. When it comes to church programs, less is more.

Evaluate your PPMs using the following steps. You can place your responses on a chart that everyone can see.

1. Make a list of your current PPMs.

2. Rate the perceived value each PPM adds to the ongoing life and ministry of your church on a scale from one to ten with ten being high.

3. Rate the perceived value each PPM adds to the fulfillment of God's vision on a scale from one to ten.

4. Rate the perceived value each PPM adds to helping you reach households in your community with the Good News from one to ten.

5. Spend some time talking and praying about your current PPMs and the role they ought to play in the future ministry of your church.

6. Rate each PPM on a scale of one to ten as to whether or not it ought to be part of the future ministry of your church.

7. From your lists develop a list of PPMs that need to be continued as is, those that must be modified and refocused in light of your vision, and those that should be stopped because they have completed their usefulness in the life and ministry of the church.

8. The final step is to determine what is missing from

the list. What new PPMs are needed to fulfil your vision. Determine how you can learn what these are and how to do them.

Some church members at the evaluation process might ask if you will now prohibit them from doing a program or activity they cherish. If your evaluation is complete, and that program did not make the cut, your answer is, "We're not saying you can't do it. We are saying we are not putting it in the budget, devoting staff time to it, or giving it a priority on the calendar. But you are free to do it."

Your most impactful processes, programs, and ministries (PPMs) are those aligned with the fulfillment of God's vision, God's full Kingdom potential for your church.

You could add, if you think it has value and is helping people, we bless you to do it, but we don't have the luxury of supporting everything people want to do. In these situations it is good to give permission.

Frazer Memorial United Methodist Church in Montgomery, AL, had gone through such a PPM evaluation. Pastor John Ed Mathison had a guideline that if a person or staff member came to him, feeling compelled by God to engage in a particular ministry or activity, John Ed wanted to hear it and bless it. For the church to get behind it with resources and calendar, the volunteer had to find five other people who had the same passion.

John Ed recalled how one woman told him she felt passion for bringing dogs, cats, and maybe birds into institutional, residential settings, such as nursing homes, retirement homes, prisons, etc. John Ed listened to her, prayed with her, and told her she needed to find other people who wanted to do it. Privately, he thought this was the dumbest idea he had ever heard. But she found people of like mind, enlisted them, started the ministry, and in several years 500 people were engaged in the PAWS ministry—Pets Are Witnessing Saints.

After this foundational exercise, focus on the three aspects of a church with D³ Intentionality. These are churches who organize their PPMs around *disciplemaking* of people rather than primarily seeking to achieve excellence around PPMs. Second, they *develop existing leaders*, while continuing to discover, recruit, and develop new leaders. Additionally, there is a bias towards *dynamic innovation execution* of new, fresh and inviting events to constantly reinvigorate a church.

Intentionally Create Sustainability

As you shift your focus from your current approach to PPMs to D³ Intentionality, consider the following continuum. Make it your goal to move your focus on PPMs from *Output* to *Impact* and from *Capacity Building* to *Sustainability*.

In the church programs world *Output* determines the matrix of success for the PPMs. How many people got involved in various processes, programs, or ministry? What was the average attendance. How many people stayed until the end and fulfilled their assignments.

Impact wants to know *about* the people who got involved in a process, program, or ministry. How many of them exhibited more Christlike understandings, attitudes, and actions? The client here is the people themselves and their involvement in a *disciplemaking* process, and not their completion of a PPM curriculum or project.

Capacity Building identifies people who have the potential to be leaders of a process, program, or ministry in which they have been engaged, and then involving them in a developing leader's journey.

Sustainability involves setting up an ongoing system to continually focus on *disciplemaking* and *developing leaders* rather than short-term projects. Sustaining the overall process must be part of *dynamic innovation execution.*

With a focus on intentionally creating sustainability, let us turn to the D³ Intentionality factors.

Disciplemaking

We hope that by now you are convinced that PPMs are all about helping people be on a spiritual and strategic journey toward living out their personal mission as fully devoted followers of Jesus. They have grown spiritually as a result of your disciplemaking process. This is your primary goal, and a PPM's success is ancillary to it.

It is about people on a pilgrimage.

Your long-term goal is for people to fully surrender their lives to God in response to His call. Helping each person discover their spiritual gifts and their Christian calling will always be more important than the PPMs. At the same time, PPMs that focus on an effective process of disciplemaking will add great value to the D³ Intentionality of your church.

———

Leadership development does not often happen without intentional action to discover, recruit, and develop leaders.

———

A multitude of disciplemaking materials are available in the Christian publishing world. Churches should examine the disiciplemaking processes to determine which ones would best fit their church. Look for materials that focus on a Christian lifestyle that emphasizes fulfilling the Great Commission in the spirit of the Great Commandment.

We are familiar with a generic disciplemaking process that outlines a progression: helping people come to *Christ*, connect with a *Congregation*, move deeply into the *Community* life of the church, come to understand their *Calling* and leadership and/or followership potential, and help them be part of God's *Commission*. The linear progression is *Christ* to *Congregation* to *Community* to *Calling* to *Commission*. However, discipleship does not always happen in this order. Each of these five phases are also entry points into a disciplemaking journey that can then involve the other phases.

Choosing the process of disciplemaking for the next stage of your congregational journey is foundational work, but it is not the most important. Remember, disciplemaking is about disciples. The most important work you will do is discovering and determining people's readiness to embark on a disciplemaking journey to become fully devoted followers of Christ. The focus should always be on making disciples who know how to make other disciples.

At the risk of having people throw hymnals at us—if your church still has hymnals—we once again say that church growth is not about developing successful processes, programs, and ministries. Church growth itself is still not the point! It is about developing committed disciples who make disciples. A happy consequence is that your church will grow as your people grow.

Developing Leaders

An important aspect of disciplemaking that deserves emphasis is developing leaders. Too many churches have too few leaders. In many leaders don't change. The ones in leadership ten years ago are still leading today. Yet these same churches complain that they do not have enough leaders. Do you see this pattern?

Leaders are growing old because the church is not growing new leaders. It is not discovering, recruiting, and developing a new generation of leaders. Any potential leaderers in the next generation have gone to another church that reconizes their leadership qualities.

D^3 Intentionality churches are always looking for the next wave or generation of leaders. Their approach is not to ask them to lead in the manner of previous leaders—the way its always been done. Rather, they seek those who will bring fresh eyes and new approaches to leadership.

Leadership development does not often happen without intentional action to discover, recruit, and develop leaders. It works the same with the leaders as it does with disciplemaking. Intentionality is essential. People making the best progress in their disciplemaking journey are probably the best prospects for leadership roles in the gathered and the scattered church.

Let us acknowledge that not everyone is called to leadership or is naturally a leader. Some people are great followers. Churches need both. One framework suggests that about 20 percent of active adults likely have a leadership calling and the capacity to serve in core leadership roles in the life of a church. Another 40 percent of active adults are ongoing or periodic followers who can help leaders accomplish their goals. Unfortunately, the final 40 percent are too passive or casual in their church commitment to serve either as a leader or a follower. Of course, there are exceptions.

This is why target efforts to discover, recruit, and develop leaders are important. In Action Four we identified a group of people known as People of Passion. These are people who have positive spiritual passion about the future to which God is pulling your church. While they might have other characteristics, spiritual passion stands out as the one they most exhibit. They may be an excellent starting point for discovering potential leaders. If these passionate ones are already leaders they will want to grow into the next level of leadership.

Another group of people in churches are known as People of Potential. These are people with leadership or followership potential, but they do not know how to get involved and no one is targeting them to a deeper role in the church. Some decades ago, these people would have volunteered for leadership or followership roles. In recent decades they are waiting to be asked. So, ask them!

Dynamic Innovative Execution

Dynamic Innovative Execution is unlike the two previous categories. It is not a group of people. It is an attitude and an action. Churches who have a positive bias to continually be innovating and executing new methodologies are likely to remain fresh in their PPMs. They will appeal to various waves of new people, and remain relevant in the continual evolution of how churches connect with their context.

Innovation is not about changing the belief system of a church. It may not even be about changing the structure of the church. It is about delivering the Good News of God's unconditional love with an ever-adapting style.

Let's say you attended an anniversary celebration of a church and then ten years later attended the same church for another anniversary. You had vivid memories of your previous visit, and you have a déjà vu moment. Everything you experienced in your previous visit was the same as this visit.

The worship service was the same. The order of the service was the same. Some of the songs were the same. The Lord's Supper or communion was administered exactly the same way. Some of the bulletin boards about the church seemed to have the same theme to them. And you noticed many other similar things.

————

Innovation is not about changing the belief system of a church. It may not even be about changing the structure of the church. It is about delivering the Good News of God's unconditional love with an ever-adapting style.

————

The only thing that seemed different is that the people were older, and there were fewer of them.

Dynamic Innovative Execution does not have to mean that radical changes take place overnight. Regular and incremental transitions and changes regularly done are sufficient and often more effective. When working with a church I (George) often suggest that rather than radically changing their worship service, leaders determine how their worship services need to change. They change one small element of the worship service every month or so until they achieve the worship experience they had envisioned. This allows time for people to adjust to and accept the transitions and changes.

Another option is to develop multiple ways to engage in various aspects of worship. Each Sunday do at least one thing different than the Sunday before. Keep worship fresh, open, and appealing. This same concept can apply to many other parts of church life and its PPMs.

I (George) visited a church in a suburban town outside a

large metropolis. The church had a beautiful sanctuary ideal for weddings, and had gained some small revenue from renting it out for weddings and funerals. The church was not doing well financially and was slowly dwindling.

Going against prevailing wisdom, a new pastor suggested the church offer a complete wedding service for free, with the stipulation that since the church was committed to Christian marriages, the marrying couple had to attend the church—or give evidence of attendance elsewhere—for at least eight weeks before the wedding. In addition, the marrying couple must attend group premarital counseling at the church.

Many couples who approached the church to host their wedding were not active in any church. Some were planning their second or third marriage and creating a blended family with children. Those who agreed to the stipulations came to the church for eight weeks before their wedding and participated in small group counseling. Virtually every time, according to the pastor, each small group became a new ongoing small group in the church.

In three years, the church grew from 100 regular attenders to more than 200. The pastor had turned a wedding venue with a wedding committee, into a missional outpost. They engaged in dynamic innovative execution.

Renewing the Core While Extending the Ministry

One concept that applies to all D^3 Intentionality factors is renewing the core while extending the ministry. It reduces process, program, and ministry busyness, and enhances disciplemaking, developing leaders, and dynamic innovative execution.

A key strategy in renewing the core is to focus on the adult heads of households. When churches are seeking to do new things, they will need more leaders and increased finances. Often churches seek to recruit people to processes, programs, and ministries however they can.

Typically, this involves doing something with children and teenage students. The problem with this approach is that these children and teenagers require leadership time and financial resources that the church can neither afford nor renew with this age group.

It used to be that the way to reach families and other households was through the children. No longer. The nuclear family as it has been traditionally defined now makes up less than ten per cent of households in North America. If you build your ministries around these traditional families using traditional methods you will miss more than nine out of ten households.

It is adult heads of households who are your future leaders and financers of your ministry. They will bring their children and teenagers with them. Your desire to draw families or households into a Christ-centered, faith-based relationship with our Triune God is genuine and authentic. But if you are not at the same time reaching at least one new head of household for every three dependent children and teenagers, your PPMs won't have enough leaders—much less leaders who are themselves on a disciplemaking journey.

To perennially extend the ministry of your church, you

must renew the core with adult heads of households who are on a disciplemaking journey, are developing as leaders, and open to dynamic innovative execution. To do anything less than this is to ultimately weaken your church. You will keep busy, but you will not be making progress.

As an example, consider a perennial program offered by thousands of churches—Vacation Bible School (VBS). Certainly, there are other summer programs that also fit this example. What is your goal for VBS? Probably to have a week of Bible curriculum and fun activities for the children of members, some of their friends, and a few children from the neighborhood. If so, it is a modified program for churched households and a few people in the community looking to get their kids out of the house.

Or is your goal to see how many children and teenagers you can entice to come to your church's VBS this week so it will be larger than last year? The fact that you do not have enough leaders and followers to do a quality job of enlistment, execution, and follow-up is not nearly as important as having bragging rights for the biggest VBS attendance in the area. (Remember the "concept of output" referenced earlier?)

Or perhaps you realize that VBS, if done well with a sufficient number of spiritually mature leaders, is one of the more effective means of evangelism through cultivation of children and teenagers. Based on your available leaders you target specific groups of children and teenagers you have been cultivating along an age and stage continuum of their spiritual journey. VBS is an additional way to help them take next steps in their pre-Christian or Christian spiritual development.

This third approach is great for renewing the core, and then extending the ministry. After several years of this approach, you can have that really large VBS week which has been your dream.

What are other areas of the processes, programs, and ministries of your church to which you can apply the concept of renewing the core while extending the ministry?

Timing Concerning Your New P3 Lead Pastor

At this point you should ask how much of the "Soar with D³ Intentionality" work needs to be done before our new P³ Lead Pastor begins his ministry at the church? And how much needs to wait until our new pastor is here?

The answer—it depends. Here are three circumstances that will affect your answer. First, in a perfect world the PPMs evaluation needs to be completed before the new pastor comes, along with any elimination of PPMs. You would not want the new pastor in the first few months' tenure to have to eliminate processes, programs, and ministries that carry emotional attachments in the church.

When the new pastor arrives the system for D³ Intentionality should be ready to start. The new pastor can use his spiritual gifts, ministerial skills, and his knowledge base to help develop the plans for *disciplemaking, developing leaders,* and engaging in *dynamic innovation execution.*

Second, if the calling of a P³ Lead Pastor is taking longer than anticipated, the church should not wait to implement

D^3 Intentionality. The church should ask their S^3 Intentional Interim Pastor to roll out the D^3 Intentionality plan to continue to create movement and capacity in the church. Annual action plans can be set for only one year ahead so the new pastor will be able to have an impact on the process soon after his arrival.

Third, if the church needs radical transition and change between pastors, it needs to engage in the D^3 Intentionality actions until the new P^3 Lead Pastor arrives. Or if it is decided that the S^3 Intentional Interim Pastor is going to remain for several years then the D^3 Intentionality actions should be engaged and completed before calling a new pastor.

CALL TO ACTION

- Engage in the evaluation exercise for your processes, programs, and ministries (PPMs).

- Consider where your church is on the continuum of Output, Impact, Capacity Building, and Sustainability, where it needs to be, and how it can get there.

- Develop plans for *disciplemaking, developing leaders,* and *dynamic innovation execution.*

- Think through ways your church can renew its core while extending its ministry.

- Determine how far you should go with D^3 Intentionality actions before your next pastor is called and has begun his ministry with your church.

CALL TO PRAYER

• Pray for your church and its leaders as it evaluates its processes, programs, and ministries and makes courageous decisions on what to stop, modify, and start.

• Pray about God's calling upon your spiritual life, and how you need to continue engaging in a disciple-making journey and develop as a leader or follower.

• Pray for the families and households you are reaching in ministry in response to God Empowering Vision.

An Incredible Year

My knuckles were white, and my grip tight on the wheel of my 2001 Hyundai Sonata. The driver and vehicle were no match for the blistering winds of an icy blizzard across the open plains of North Dakota.

Every time I looked in my rearview mirror, I saw a tractor-trailer barreling up behind me on Interstate 94. Snow was blowing horizontally with the whipping, snapping winds. Ice was forming beneath my wipers. Truck after truck closed in on me, looking like they were going to drive right over me before they suddenly veered and passed to my left. Their wake blinded me in a whiteout. I peered through the blanket of snow and followed the truck's taillights disappearing into the night until the road reappeared. The color would then return to my knuckles.

This harrowing experience went on for 400 miles. I was grateful to have a traveling companion, Sparty, my Kerry Blue Terrier and a good friend in any circumstance.

I was on my way to a small church in Hardin, Montana, that needed an Interim Pastor. This church was my first assignment with IPM, and, other than Sparty, I was on my own as my wife stayed behind in Milwaukee for work and to care for her aged mother. My start date was the fourth Sunday of Advent. When Sparty and I finally made it to Hardin, the former pastor still occupied the parsonage, so we checked into the Super 8.

For me, Advent and joy always go together. This year was different. Only 28 people showed up for the final Sunday of Advent. They were discouraged; yet, I was hopeful.

The first step in the IPM process is connecting with people. An old church directory and Clara helped me do just that. Clara knew everyone and where they lived. Soon we were making phone calls, and Clara gave me directions to places beyond my GPS's reach. When making a "getting to know you" visit in eastern Montana, I soon discovered that I must always have a full gas tank. One wrong turn can take your gas gauge down by a quarter.

For the next three months, I called on everyone who had been a part of the church. Sometimes, I made a wrong turn and ended up at a stranger's house. Rather than be frustrated, I would introduce myself, tell them who I was looking for, and then share my faith story with them.

Back at the church, warmth began to seep into the walls and rafters. Former members returned, and new people came to check us out. I began preaching a series on hearing God's voice and what it means to be God's people. I had a transition team in no time, and new life sprigs began budding in the church.

The transition team completed a significant self-study with a clear vision for reaching children and youth. We acted on the plan, and the first action was clearing the Christian education wing of junk. When we discovered some fantastic art from a very old Sunday School curriculum, we framed and displayed it.

In my local travels, I noticed many people had e-waste (TVs, computers, printers, copiers, cell phones, video games), but there was no place for disposal. We did an e-waste fundraiser on Earth Day to send kids to summer camp. One weekend, we gathered two tons of e-waste, raised $4,000, and made the local paper's front page. That summer, we sent many kids to Bethel Bible Camp in the Little Big Horn Mountains of Wyoming.

When new families began coming, I added a children's message to the service. Our VBS that summer was a huge success. A picture of kids overflowing the church became the cover for our new church directory.

With fall just around the corner, we took our Evangelical Catechism into the twenty-first century by setting up an interactive classroom. We ordered new student tables with fun swivel chairs and hung whiteboards and bulletin boards. We provided each student with a laptop computer. We bought a printer and buzzer system for Bible quizzing. Students made their own Bible memory cards and question-and-answer cards from the Catechism. That year, there was a large confirmation class.

Little by little, joy began returning to the people, and the church began to fill up. The former pastor moved on, and trustees refurbished the parsonage. Fall was slipping by. All the kids loved Sparty, and the people loved me. The Advent season was soon upon us, and the church was full of warmth. By now, our weekly attendance had grown from 40 to 100.

One year to the date of my arrival and on the fourth Sunday of Advent, we introduced our new pastor to the church. I brought out a huge box wrapped in bright Christmas paper with a large red bow on top to say goodbye. Unknown to all, the new pastor's youngest son, Jackson, hid inside.

I called everyone upfront, asking them to guess what was in the box. Then, tapping the box, I quoted Ephesians 4:11 saying that He gave His Church gifts: some to be apostles, some to be prophets and evangelists, and some to be pastors and teachers.

I then tipped the box and out jumped Jackson to everyone's surprise. I gathered Jackson in front of me and said that God had given us a pastor and his family this year. They are gifts from Jesus to His Church. And we are to love them and value them as gifts from above.

That Sunday, there were 145 people in the church. I handed a baton to our new pastor. My trip home with Sparty was a breeze.

Call a P³ Lead Pastor
Continue to Soar
Far and High

How would your church define a passionate,
proactive, and personable P³ Lead Pastor for your
unique situation?

———

How does what you have learned as a C³ Soaring
Church seeking to fulfill God's Empowering Vision with
D³ Intentionality inform the pastoral search process?

———

What does an excellent P³ Lead Pastor
search process look like?

———

Who are the best people in your church to serve
on the PST?

———

How will you know when you have found the
P³ Lead Pastor for your church?

———

By now your church is already benefiting from the interim period and soaring between pastors. You have grown in your understanding of who you are and addressed elephants in the room. You have launched a strategic prayer initiative and reflected on your church in the context of New Testament churches. You have evaluated processes, programs, and ministries in the absence of personality issues. You have paused to celebrate the new life reaching for sunlight in your congregation.

You have worked hard to become a C³ Soaring Church and are ready to discover the P³ Lead Pastor God has prepared for you. You are seeking to fulfill your God Empowering Vision through D³ Intentionality with strategies for *disciplemaking, developing leaders,* and *dynamic innovative execution.*

A P³ Lead Pastor is passionate about the Good News of Jesus the Christ and is gifted in preaching and teaching about the Good News. *Proactivity* characterizes a P³ Lead Pastor, especially in the areas of vision casting and fulfillment, and the development of disciples prepared to serve as leaders in and through the church. It is highly important for a P³ Lead Pastor to be *personable.* It should be obvious that they love being with people and encouraging them as disciples and nurturing them through life stages of predictable and unpredictable life events.

Lets look in detail at what characterizes a pastor who is *passionate, proactive,* and *personable* and qualifies them as a P³ Lead Pastor.

First, a pastor who is passionate about the Good News of Jesus Christ exhibits a genuine, authentic, and maturing relationship with God through Jesus Christ. The number one priority in their lives is their spiritual relationship with our Triune God. It is obvious that they love the Lord. They have a faith that captivates their heart, soul, mind, and strength.

They don't carry a "holier than thou" attitude. They are not aloof or out of touch. It is evident that they love the Lord and the people they serve. Spend any amount of time with a

P³ Lead Pastor and you will soon realize their authenticity comes from knowing Christ and walking with Him. They lead by example, both in the church and its ministry context.

A P³ Lead Pastor's sphere of influence is not limited to their church. They want everyone to have a Christ-centered, faith-based relationship with God through Jesus Christ, to grow in the grace and knowledge of our Lord, and to share in word and deed their faith with others. While they love the Christian Church and will cherish and seek to help your church reach its full Kingdom potential, they know the most important thing is the spiritual relationship of every person with our Heavenly Father.

Additionally, this pastor's passion is clearly present when they preach and teach the Good News. While they should not be expected to preach like some wellknown superstar pastor, it is obvious they have above average communication skills. They can clearly and simply present biblical truths, illustrate real life applications of God's Word to the church, and apply doctrinal understandings to daily life.

Second, a pastor who is proactive is excited to lead a church that is already in movement instead of at rest. They love that the church has focused on the *Great Commission* in the spirit of the *Great Commandment*, and enduring core values, as well as being captured by God's Empowering Vision during the interim between pastors. They look forward to helping the church cast God's vision and focus efforts on fulfilling this vision as they live into it.

They rejoice when the Pastoral Search Team (PST) does

not say to them, "Come help us find vision!" but is able to say, "This is the vision we believe God has for us. Does that align with God's call upon your ministry?" At the same time, a proactive pastor realizes they must listen, learn, and discern the church's heart for the vision and its commitment to intentionally live into it.

———

A proactive pastor looks for laypersons who love the Lord and their walk with Him even more than they love their church.

———

They know that churches can learn the right words to say, but it is inspired action that is most important. They will test the PST to find out if their words and commitment to living into God's Empowering Vision are deeply and broadly affirmed throughout the church. Many pastors have arrived in their new church only to discover the PST sold them on a commitment that was not characteristic of the church as a whole. Be ready for your test.

A proactive pastor looks for laypersons who love the Lord and their walk with Him even more than they love their church. They understand the difference between being a maturing disciple and being a faithful church member. Disciplemaking is their ultimate task. Maturing disciples are also proactive leaders and followers. A pastoral candidate who is proactive will look for evidence that the church wants to be led to places of higher service in God's Kingdom rather than to call a passive pastor who keeps the church satisfied.

Third, a pastor who is personable is a joy to be around. This has nothing to do with their charisma or popularity. It has everything to do with how much they like people and enjoy talking with them, and listening to them with an open and discerning heart. Pastoral care is a meaningful part of their ministry. You would recommend them to people facing spiritual and other life crises.

Personable pastors are approachable. They connect well with church leaders, the average person in the congregation, and with new people curious about Jesus and your church. They do not have a simple answer to all of life's complexities, but they are interested in helping people find the resources to work through the joys and sorrows of life. It is obvious they are eager to see you grow in the grace and knowledge of our Lord.

They are clearly a non-anxious presence in the midst of the crises. Even a pandemic does not derail their personable ministry focus. They know how to network people to embrace opportunities and to speak into challenges a church faces.

It is important for your church to understand several things about P³ Lead Pastors. First, they are just like you in many ways. That is, they have not reached their full potential in the three areas of being *passionate*, *proactive*, and *personable*. They will work on growing in these leadership capacities for the rest of their ministry.

Second, they are not equally gifted and skilled in all of the P³ characteristics. Some are only truly strong in one or two of the three characteristics. But if they are aware of this, they are working on the others. Few are strong in all three.

One of the best things your church can do for your next P³ Lead Pastor is to give them opportunity to focus on their own growth. Allow them annual time away for continuing education. Give them a generous number of vacation days including Sundays off. Provide a budget to work with a coach, mentor, or participate in a peer learning community as they seek guidance in adjusting their spiritual gifts and ministerial skills to best serve your congregation.

Doing so will allow them to serve you longer as pastor, as they deepen and broaden ministerial capacities. It will also help them maintain their spiritual and emotional health.

Once you understand the characteristics of a P³ Lead Pastor, it is time to begin in earnest the search for God's next pastor for your church. This search could be the most crucial action your church will take in the next decade. The work of your PST bears a great responsibility to God's Kingdom, to the church, to your ministry context, and to the future pastor and his family.

PST members must be in a current season of spiritual growth, seeking to know God's heart and to hear His voice which can only come from an intimate love relationship with Him.

The Bible says in Proverbs 3:5-6 that we are to "Trust in the Lord with all your heart and lean not on your understanding; in all your ways acknowledge Him, and He will make your paths straight." The success, effectiveness, and timeframe of this pastoral search are directly related to the PST's spiritual fitness, commitment, process, and due diligence.

The Foundation for a Pastoral Search Process

It is hard to resist launching your pastoral search prematurely. It is crucial to lay a foundation for the pastoral search. This takes time and patience to work through an intentional interim process.

Your S³ Intentional Interim Pastor has helped you navigate the landmines that lay just under the surface. And remove them. Your new pastor should not be stepping on landminnes and damaging his ministry before it starts. The interim pastor should not let the church move into the pastoral search phase until he has helped the leadership to address and resolve critical issues. The failure to resolve challenges before a new pastor's call guarantees preexisting issues will sabotage and prematurely end his ministry.

The Pastor Profile

When you have resolved issues and clarified the church's mission, core values, and vision, you are ready to formulate a pastor profile. This profile is a composite picture of the characteristics the church seeks in a P³ Lead Pastor. A well-written profile that genuinely represents the consensus of the church's leadership and the vision helps the PST with the leadership and the congregation. Such an agreement ensures that everyone is on the same page as the PST looks for a P³ Lead Pastor.

The size of your PST should be large enough to offer a variety of perspectives but not so large that it is unwieldy.

Without such a guiding document, it is too easy—and too tempting—for individual team members' personal preferences to drive the search. If a PST member or two are working to secure a different pastor from the agreed-upon pastor profile, a division can crop up. If a new pastor discovers that the church's culture and identity are nothing like the search committee portrayed it, his tenure will be short, and many lives will be in spiritual and emotional disarray.

Pastor profiles typically include a description of the pastor's character qualities, education, and experience preferences, plus denominational allegiance. The profile also consists of the desired spiritual gifts and personal attributes, the needed competencies and skills, the essential doctrinal beliefs and theological positions, and the church's desired preaching style.

Given the changing church landscape and shrinking opportunities for full-time pastor openings, it is common for a church to receive many pastoral recommendations and applications. The search team qualifies or disqualifies applicants by comparing the inquiring pastors against the pastor profile. Knowing the kind of pastor the search team wants focuses their time and energy on the best candidates.

I (Tom) saw one sizeable healthy church receive hundreds of resumes. This enormous pile of resumes could have bogged them down for months. Using the pastor profile as a screener, the search team quickly sent regrets letters to over 90 percent of the applicants.

Selecting a Pastoral Search Team

Employ great wisdom and discretion in selecting the PST. You are entrusting them to identify the person who will become your P³ Lead Pastor. They present the final candidate the church will be asked to affirm.

These team members should be of strong Christian character, faithfulness, and commitment to the church, and possess a high degree of spiritual discernment. Have you included your core opinion leaders? The team should consist of both men and women and a range of ages. Check with the church's governing documents for the team composition requirements, including any required church leadership roles. Include those who have excellent relational and communication skills because the team will need to regularly communicate and interact with candidates, references, and a curious congregation.

The size of your PST should be large enough to offer a variety of perspectives but not so large that it is unwieldy. Seven to nine members is an ideal size, with an odd number of members for voting purposes. The PST should seek to reach a unanimous consensus in its final decisions about a candidate.

Training the Pastoral Search Team

Devote the first meetings of the PST to building relationships between team members. Then train them in their roles and the dynamics of the PST. Provide each team member with a copy of a pastoral search book to read and discuss. I (Tom) highly recommend *"Help We Just Lost Our Pastor! A Step by Step Guide for Pastoral Transitions"* by Ken Moberg (NextStep Resources).

You will need to establish some ground rules that all members agree to follow throughout the search process. At the top of that list is the need for absolute confidentiality. You owe it to each candidate and your church to maintain confidentiality. One leak on social media can start a wildfire of rumors and speculation that can damage the candidate's relationship with his current church. Do not assume that the need for confidentiality is understood. Address it plainly and make it a priority.

The interim pastor should connect the team with denominational networks and tools for a pastoral search. He should invite the denomination's area leader to meet with the team early in the search process to speak about the denomination's placement processes, expectations, and resources. If geographical distance is an issue, use videoconferencing.

If the denomination has a prescribed process for accessing candidates within its databases, the interim pastor must become familiar with it. He will want to follow the denomination's search steps to guide the team's compliance. Many regional denominational leaders will want to meet with the search team to explain their search processes and resources.

For example, the Evangelical Free Church of America (EFCA) utilizes a Pastoral Search Program. This program matches pastors with churches by comparing candidate pro-files with open positions at churches throughout the EFCA. Converge Worldwide (formerly the Baptist General Confer-ence) has its own Placement Program with its unique pro-cesses and resources.

How the Interim Pastor Should Interact with the Pastoral Search Team

A reminder: Your leadership and the interim pastor should have agreed at the beginning of the interim pastor's service that he is *not* a candidate for permanent pastor. Your interim pastor's only agenda is the church's health and vitality. Because he cannot be a candidate for your permanent position, he will not position himself to be your next pastor. Therefore, he can be open, honest, and speak the truth in love.

By the time the pastoral search commences, the interim pas-tor will have invested a great deal of himself into the church and deeply care about finding God's P³ Lead Pastor. In coach-ing the PST, the wise and mature interim pastor will be care-ful not to influence the search process and selection. Wielding too much influence could weaken the new pastor's legitimacy. People might perceive the interim pastor chose him.

The interim pastor must guard himself against going beyond the limits of his role. He cannot chair the PST or act as *de facto* chair. He should not be a voting member of the group or do anything that could suggest he is misusing his influence to secure his desired candidate's selection. Instead, the interim pastor will best serve the team and the church if he acts as a coach—training, guiding, advising, and encouraging the team through the pastoral search process.

As a good coach, he will help team members discover and appreciate the spiritual gifts and natural talents they bring to the process. He will help the team know what to anticipate,

---

A pastor's ability to manage his emotions and control his reactions is essential to his leadership. An emotionally stable pastor walks wisely and leads well through conflicts and challenges.

---

and educate and train the team in best practices and potential challenges of a pastoral search. He can offer encouragement when it is needed.

If your chosen candidate withdraws his name and your second-choice candidate has already taken a church, it is disheartening. A good coach encourages a team after a severe loss with his presence, guidance, and prayers. Like a good coach, he entrusts the team captain with increasing responsibilities, provides him the resources and knowledge he needs to lead, and publicly supports him. The interim pastor does everything he can to enable the search chair to lead the team well.

Identifying P3 Lead Pastor Traits

A good coach recognizes the many distractions that cause his team to lose focus. Similarly, members of a PST can get distracted by any number of things: a flood of questions and opinions, pressure from church members to hurry up, the appearance and personality style of candidates, and by their varied preferences and anxieties. The interim pastor must keep the team focused on the essential qualities they are looking for in a P³ Lead Pastor.

A pastor's *character* is ultimately more important than his training, experience, eloquence, or charisma. Evaluate every potential pastoral candidate by the character qualities in 1 Timothy 3 and Titus 1. Use sermon samples, virtual and face-to-face interviews, and reference checks to go even deeper.

An often-overlooked area of character is the candidate's emotional and relational maturity, which Ken Sande—the founder of Peacemaker Ministries—calls relational wisdom. A pastor's ability to manage his emotions and control his reactions is essential to his leadership. An emotionally stable pastor walks wisely and leads well through conflicts and challenges.

A pastor's *competency* is key to his long-term fruitfulness at a church. It cannot be evaluated solely on what he writes on a resume. Ideally, the interim pastor has helped church leaders determine the primary core competencies they are looking for in P³ Lead Pastor as part of the pastor profile. Those core competencies commonly include preaching, teaching, and pastoral care. Others would include administration, leadership development, visioning, and more.

Chemistry describes how the candidate will fit the church's culture and how he relates to the staff and church leadership. The PST can evaluate some of this by ensuring their interviewing and reference checking processes explore the candidate's leadership style, philosophy of ministry, and personal preferences.

To better understand the applicant, consider using personality, and spiritual gift assessment tools. I (Tom) recommend Myers-Briggs, DiSC®, and Uniquely You—which combines a spiritual gift assessment with a DiSC® assessment—to further evaluate the candidate's potential fit.

When the timing in the search process is right, the PST should bring a candidate to the church for a confidential visit. Introduce the prospective pastor through formal and informal meetings with the search team, key church staff, and the church's governing group. You learn much about a candidate's personality and his potential fit from spending time with him and his spouse over meals, driving him around town, and other informal activities.

Carefully evaluate the pastor's capacity to handle the church's size, staff needs, leadership's structure, and the congregation's culture and denomination. Pastor and author Tim Keller says one of the most common reasons for pastoral selection missteps and mistakes is blindness to the significance of church size. A church's size profoundly affects decision-making processes, relational flow, job descriptions, and ministry effectiveness of pastors, staff, and lay leaders.

The PST should consider how a candidate's pastoral experience will help him have a basic understanding of the culture and size of the church. This understanding will help him avoid the related mistakes and missteps that would weaken his leadership and potentially lead to an early exit.

It's critical the pastor has a clear sense of *calling*, both to pastoral ministry and even to this church. Ask, "Why are you a pastor"? Explore your candidate's journey of faith, including what led him into pastoral ministry. Press him to explain his calling to this church. Ask him what about this particular opportunity excites him and makes him think he would be a good fit.

Be careful with pastors who are not presently serving in pastoral ministry. There may be an underlying sense of desperation motivating their interest in your church. You also want to investigate the reason why they are not serving at present.

It is vitally important to discern how *collaborative* a candidate would be in his leadership. Too many pastors leave their churches prematurely because they have become embroiled in power struggles with church leadership or staff. Pastor's models often conflict with the church leadership's model. This conflict happens most often when the pastor and the governing board are at odds over who discerns and drives the church's vision and implementation. Precisely define the role of the leadership group, the lead pastor, and the congregants. This includes the power and authority inherent to that role.

When the church's leadership structure is a pyramid with either the pastor or the governing group at its apex, the resulting struggles for control inevitably produce conflict. A collaborative leadership is healthier for the church. The pastor and leadership collaborate in discerning God's will and vision for the church. In a small church, the pastor, governing group, and lay leaders will implement the vision. In a medium to large church, the lead pastor and staff implement the vision and action plans.

The Search Process

It will help the church to see a timeline showing the search team's process and expectations. Setting estimates and goals for each stage helps the group function effectively, and encourages the rest of the church. That timeline begins with the PST starting to meet weekly. The first month should focus on their training and connecting with denominational networks.

In the first few meetings, team members should choose a chairperson and vice-chairperson. A secretary or recorder maintains necessary correspondence with candidates. Hopefully, someone on the team can navigate online resources to post the position opening and obtain web-based materials on potential applicants.

Because the pastoral search should be born out of and sustained by fervent prayer, the team would be wise to appoint a prayer coordinator. This prayer leader will keep both the team and the congregation focused on regular, strategic, and sustained pastoral search prayer. The prayer coordinator will seek guidance from the team in relaying prayer requests and updates.

Have you drafted a church profile? What can a candidate learn about your church? A church profile combines information from the congregational survey, the church's history, governance, core values, vision, ministries, staff, lay leadership, and facilities. Synthesize and compile this information into a document that will help interested candidates begin to discern whether they would potentially fit into the next season of the church's ministry.

A community profile provides interested candidates with necessary information about the community the church serves. Include your community's demographic makeup, business base, schools, and opportunities for housing and recreation.

Some PSTs combine their church profile and community profile into one attractive brochure. It can be made available online at the church's website or emailed as an attachment to interested candidates.

You are now ready to post the position. If the church is part of a denomination, post with its placement networks and affiliated seminaries. You can also post with other placement networks as well as seminaries deemed compatible with the church's doctrine and beliefs. Compensation websites are options.

The PST should set up a dedicated email account to receive all application materials and other inquiries. All applicants should make all contacts with the church through that email account.

A well-prepared launch of the position opening will typically produce a quick flow of resumes from applicants. It is crucial to develop a system for collecting and filing the resumes, acknowledging receipt of their information to applicants, and providing copies to all the team members. This information flow can become overwhelming in a hurry.

Do not assume you must select your P³ Lead Pastor from that initial group of applicants. In many cases, God's timing in identifying a P³ Lead Pastor will test the team's patience and commitment. The best practice is to review, and rate resumes as they are received. Eliminate those who do not meet the criteria and send these applicants a kind note of regret expressing appreciation for their interest. Too many churches neglect this step. Don't leave pastor applicants hanging as they pray and seek God's will. Respond to every applicant promptly, clearly, and with their interests in mind.

When a resume meets your profile criteria, you should consider that candidate at the next team meeting. Many teams ask candidates to submit preaching samples at this point and find that access to online videos of a candidate's sermons is most helpful to evaluate his preaching.

For those who have made it past the first cut and rate as top candidates, ask them to complete a written questionnaire that delves into their ministry practices, doctrinal positions, and previous experience. If the team likes what they see from the preaching samples and questionnaire responses, schedule the first interview by video conference.

At this point, any serious candidate will want to know some detailed information about the church. They may want to see a copy of the church governing documents, your vision and strategic plan, history, annual report which, includes the budget. Be careful about revealing the budgeted package for the pastor. For your top two to five candidates, you should, however, provide them ballpark numbers to gauge if the compensation meets their financial needs and requirements.

Be honest. If you present a picture that does not accurately reflect who you are, you are setting yourself up to choose the wrong candidate. You are setting the candidate and his family up for a huge disappointment.

If all these steps have yielded a top candidate, bring him and his wife to the church for a visit. Get the PST together with them over dinner. You might include the church leadership group. Spend time getting to know them and ask more in-depth questions. During the visit, show them around your church facility and drive them around your ministry context.

Some teams choose their top two or three candidates for such visits. Other teams consider each candidate one at a time, inviting them to visit when the search team has narrowed their search down to that candidate. We recommend working with one candidate at a time.

Depending upon the church's policies, these visits can also include an initial interview with the church's governing group and an opportunity to meet the church's staff. It would be best if you had started your reference checks by this point.

The exciting day will finally come when the PST reaches a consensus on the person they want to call to be their P³ Lead Pastor. If the church leadership has not yet met the candidate, the interim pastor can help them complete any final interviewing they believe necessary before extending the candidate an invitation to come to the church for a candidate weekend.

Ideally, the candidate and his entire family will spend several days at the church meeting and interacting with the congregation members, staff, and leadership and teaching and preaching in several forums. Plan a schedule that will provide maximum exposure to the candidate without overloading him and his family.

Suppose the church's governance requires members to vote on a candidate to become its pastor. In that case, that vote should be scheduled either at the end of that weekend or within the next day or two so the candidate can promptly receive and respond to the official call to become the church's pastor.

Congratulations! May your pastoral search be a process that blesses your entire congregation as you seek and find a match that you will eventually describe as a match made in heaven. May your new P³ Lead Pastor serve God and your church for many years with great faithfulness, effectiveness, and innovation. May your church soar in the fulfillment of God's Empowering Vision during his tenure.

CALL TO ACTION

- As part of your pastor profile developed by the Pastoral Search Team, clearly define what a passionate, proactive, and personable P³ Lead Pastor looks like for your unique situation.

- Consider carefully what you have learned from crafting a C³ Soaring Church and a D³ Intentionality movement. This should inform your search for a P³ Lead Pastor.

- Carefully consider—as the Pastoral Search Team— your criteria for identifying the P³ Lead Pastor for your church.

CALL TO PRAYER

- Pray without ceasing for the work of the Pastoral Search Team.

- Pray without ceasing for the P^3 Lead Pastor God is calling as your next pastor.

- Pray without ceasing that the whole church may be soaring between pastors and not passively waiting for the next pastor to come.

Preparing for "Pastor Right" When Everything Went Wrong

First Church was on a roll. Their pastor had dynamic communication gifts and a charismatic personality. Attendance was growing, giving was strong, and the church added a new campus across town.

The church was shocked to learn that he had been in an ongoing immoral sexual relationship with a staff member. On Sunday, he preached a stirring message on Romans 8, and on Friday he commited suicide by hanging himself from the balcony of his home.

To compound the tragedy, 60 days later, the very beloved No. 2 pastor died of cancer.

As the incoming interim pastor, I found the church deeply grieving after two heartbreaking funerals. The question "Why?" was being asked on multiple levels. The church had lost momentum as they sat under a dark cloud of broken trust and uncertainty.

A congregation suffering this kind of trauma needs time to grieve in a safe, comforting and reassuring environment. An interim pastor can provide stable spiritual leadership to create this environment for the congregation and staff, and give the church time to heal and prepare to receive a new pastor.

After nine months, the elders sensed it was time to begin the search process. Over those months I provided four critical inputs.

1. SELECT EACH TEAM MEMBER

I advised them to select individuals for the PST who had gone through a difficult season of trusting the Lord. The search for a Lead Pastor is typically a marathon and an emotional rollercoaster. You want people on the search team who have learned to trust the Lord when the way forward isn't straightforward or easy.

2. IDENTIFY THE PERSON FOR WHOM YOU'RE LOOKING

Early in the process, I had the search team meet with the elder board. I had them make three lists: Gotta Have (non-negotiable items); Want to Have (essential elements); Would Like to Have (helpful but not necessary). Building this profile at the front end prevents the search team from presenting a candidate who is not a fit for the church.

3. DESIGN THE PROCESS

Before the search goes public, the team does the hard work of designing a candidate evaluation process. What are the steps to take with each applicant? For example: Where will we look for applicants? What filters will we use? Who receives and evaluates the resumes? What questions are essential in the interview process? When is it time to speak on the phone or have video calls? When do we get face-to-face? Will all our decisions along the way need to be unanimous or a majority?

4. START DATING

I repeatedly reminded the search team that the best analogy for what they're doing is a dating relationship that leads to marriage. The initial attraction may come from outward appearance, but the heart reveals the lasting character of a lifetime commitment. The initial questions are the easy "get-to-know-you" type, but vulnerability and trust must eventually develop to explore competence, integrity, and chemistry issues so that both parties can know if this is a "fit".

The search process at First Church took a year. The search team received over 500 responses to the posted position. The filters screened that overwhelming number down to 150 resumes to seriously consider.

Over time, I watched as the search process sharpened the team's ability to ask the right questions, quickly perceive an applicant's fit, and learn to trust each other's discernment.

When the Lord finally brought the person who would eventually become the next pastor, it didn't take long for the search team to recognize his potential fit for the church. Excitement grew as they spent personal time with the candidtate and his wife. When the search team explained to the elders why they were recommending the candidate, the elders quickly saw how the process revealed him as a great fit—an insight confirmed by the entire church, which wholeheartedly embraced him as their new pastor.

Engage an S³ Intentional Interim Pastor

Connect with a Sully

Is an S³ Intentional Interim Pastor right for your church?

———

What will it look like to have an S³ Intentional Interim Pastor serving your church?

———

Do you have a strong enough desire to soar between pastors that you are willing to engage in the actions recommended in this book?

———

Do you have the patience and assurance of God's leadership to engage in the transitions and changes necessary to soar between pastors?

———

What if the pilot in control of US Airways Flight 1549 on January 15, 2009 was less than a Sully Sullenberger? What if this was their first time as captain of an Airbus A320? What if they had never flown out of New York's LaGuardia Airport and were not familiar with Teterboro Airport enough to know they could not make it? What if the whole idea of landing on the Hudson River had been a crazy thought to them?

Thankfully, this didn't happen because that flight was

piloted by Sully. We want your church to be connected with an S³ Intentional Interim Pastor (S³) and ultimately a P³ Lead Pastor who have Sully qualities.

A great way to transition from your former pastor to your next pastor is to use the services of an S³ who is seasoned, skilled, and strategic. An S³ is not a newbie. They can help your church thrive between pastors. What does it mean for a S³ to be *seasoned*, *skilled*, and *strategic*?

Seasoned: An S³ is seasoned because the challenging work of an intentional interim is not for novices. It requires many years of fruitful ministry working with leaders, staff, and congregants. Intentional Interim Pastors are seasoned in leading churches to reach their full Kingdom potential. The lessons learned and wisdom gleaned from many years of pastoral experience are necessary and invaluable. They will seldom encounter a church situation they have not experienced before.

Have you ever been on a diet for various health reasons that didn't allow seasoning? Or, perhaps in your hurry to cook a meal you forgot to add seasoning? Yeah, us too. The food was bland. Not satisfying. It left us wanting something better.

A seasoned S³ is not bland. He is satisfying. He does not leave you wanting. He has been around many different church situations throughout his ministry. He is accomplished, knowledgeable, and mature enough to understand your church's potential during the interim between pastors.

As I (George) was writing this my wife, who was out delivering food to a sick family, sent me a text. She was going to stop by a certain restaurant and pick up some soup for our lunch and wanted to know if the chicken tortilla soup at the restaurant was seasoned mild, medium, or hot. I said medium. She brought home the soup, and as we began to eat it, we both realized it was much too spicy for us. I told her they must have changed their chef, their recipe, or both.

An S³ is appropriately seasoned. He will not shock or strongly agitate your church. He knows it would not be appropriate to push the church to do something for which they are not ready. He does not have a personal agenda that might overwhelm your church. He seeks to help you be reimaged in God's image and not his image.

Most importantly, he is seasoned enough to fend off requests from some people in the church who ask him to be their next pastor. He knows not only that it is inappropriate, but that it will also circumvent the search process and likely cause unhealthy conflict in the church.

S³s know how to bring help and hope to a grieving and conflicted church. They know how to discover and address the issues that have kept your church from soaring like an eagle. Perhaps the best word to characterize a seasoned S³ is "wise". Wisdom applied to difficult circumstances yields good results. An S³ exercises wisdom in his relationships with and leadership of your church to bring about the best result possible. You will appreciate that he is suitably seasoned as a minister.

Skilled: Churches in transition need interim pastors trained in transitional church issues, processes, and tasks. S³ interims have above average ministerial *skills* and will be able to skillfully lead the church during the transition between pastors.

Serving as an Intentional Interim Pastor is a unique call within God's constellation of spiritual calls. An S³ interim is self-aware enough to know what skills they have and those they do not have. Where there are gaps, they have sought additional training, coaching, or mentoring to help them develop the skillful practices necessary to serve as an Intentional Interim Pastor.

A Word of Caution

When you look for an interim pastor watch out for two things. First, be careful of hiring an interim who has attended an interim pastor training "mill." Serving as an interim pastor is popular among retired or convocational ministers. To acquire some of the skills needed, they may engage in a certification process offered by many denominations, seminaries, and parachurch organizations.

For some of these, the training and certifying of interim pastors is a good money-maker. They turn out a lot of graduates. But the process can be easily compromised or manipulated. It can become a *good ol' boy* scenario. The training organization does not necessarily assess the readiness of their graduates. Their assessment is comprised of paying the fee and attending the classes. Therefore, do not automatically assume that the graduate of any training program meets the standard of an S³ Intentional Interim Pastor.

There are, of course, certified interim pastors who are excellent at their job. Churches learn of their reputation and seek them out when they are ending one church interim and ready to move to the next.

I (George) know a highly skilled interim pastor who went through a certain certification process. His first three interims were all churches I knew well. I had been a member of the first church he served, and my sister was a member at the second church. I had led the third church through conflict mediation and strategic planning process about 15 years earlier.

As each of the churches came to the point of calling a P³ Lead Pastor, I hoped and prayed that this exceptional interim would be one to prepare them. I had nothing to do with recommending or placing this person in this succession of three churches. God handled that. In all three he served them with great grace, style, and effectiveness.

At the same time, the place where he trained—while offering excellent content—did not take the time or effort to effectively assess their students. I have often said about this institution that I hoped that 80 percent of their graduates would never serve a church as interim. Their graduates were generally ineffective ministers. That is why it's important to know the interim candidate well and get referrals where possible. This particular interim was the exception, already exceptional when he began their training.

The second thing to watch out for are interim pastor candidates who were not effective when they were in full-time ministry. Their churches did not grow in relationship to the ministry context they were serving. They were not exceptional P³ Lead Pastors during their most active years of ministry. Regardless of who recommends them, your church

----

Serving as an Intentional Interim Pastor is a unique call within God's constellation of spiritual calls.

----

should do a credible ministry background check of any interim pastor candidate you are considering.

A caveat. It's true that some ministers are better interim pastors than they are long-term pastors, even as some ministers are better church planters than they are long-term pastors of established churches. The gifts, skills, and preferences of ministers vary widely. This is why the third-party assessment of an interim candidate is so important.

A *skilled* interim pastor knows how to activate the church to take courageous steps to maximize their strengths and address their weaknesses. Be sure this is true of the person you are asking to serve as a S³ interim.

Strategic: To be effective, an S³ interim must be *strategic*. *Strategic* actions that help the church make progress in the interim come naturally to them. S³ interims do not mark time or make things up as they go. They are intentional and strategic in their approach. They help the church celebrate strengths and use these strengths to address challenges. They know how to engage your church to discover and discern its mission, core values, vision, and strategies for the forthcoming decade. They may help you stop things that are no longer effective and start processes, programs, and ministries that align with your vision.

S³ interims don't simply help you plan. They also provide

readiness activities that will help your chuch prepare for planning. All of this is strategic and helps set your church up for success in the short term - the next one to three years—and for the long term future. Through a spiritual and strategic process, the church is refreshed and refashioned in keeping with God's design for your church.

While a church might not get everything it needs during the interim, an S³ Intentional Interim Pastor can lead a church through this leg of the relay and pass the baton to the new P³ Lead Pastor. With the church relationally, spiritually, and organizationally renewed, the next pastor has the best chance to have a long and fruitful ministry.

Is Your Church Ready for an S³ Intentional Interim Pastor?

In an ideal world, every church is a pearl of great value and desiring of an S³ Intentional Interim Pastor. Not every church, however, wants the premium services of an S³ interim. They just want to get a new pastor as soon as possible.

Particularly if the former pastor left as a result of conflict, a church may want a short interim period so they can get over the pain of the past few weeks or months. They falsely believe if they get a new pastor that everything will be fine. They do not realize they are setting themselves up to repeat the conflict within a few years. The 12 to 18 months following the termination of a pastor, or a church split, will determine the long-term pattern of a church. An S³ interim can significantly increase the chances of a healthy future for a church.

Some churches are in denial about how mediocre or at-risk they are. They do not realize they need to address spiritual and strategic issues so that they can reach God's full Kingdom potential for them. Status quo is good enough for them. It's good enough to have someone fill the pulpit for a while until they can get their next pastor.

Other churches see the interim period as a time to save money and build up a financial reserve. They know that having an S³ interim will not save them money. They want to get

---

S³ Interims don't simply help you plan. They also provide readiness activities that will help your church prepare for planning.

---

by as cheaply as they can during the interim period. Often the people pushing this perspective are not tithers, but those who give just enough to keep the church functioning. There may even be some people who have an issue with tithing, and see the interim period as a time they will not have to give as much money to the church.

Readiness Questions: Providing examples of churches who are not ready for an S³ interim is informative. But its not as helpful as having your leadership consider the characteristics of readiness for an S³ Intentional Interim Pastor at your church.

1. Your church may need an S³ Intentional Interim Pastor if you realize that your former pastor left because of conflict in the church. You know you must deal with this conflict

before you call your next pastor.

2. Your church may need an S³ Intentional Interim Pastor if you realize that the loss of your former pastor—due to his illness or his death—caused deep grief and pain. You need time and processes for healing before you call your next pastor.

3. Your church may need an S³ Intentional Interim Pastor if the context your church serves has been changing racially, ethnically, and socioeconomically. Your church realizes it must refocus its ministry to be effective in your setting before you call your next pastor.

4. Your church may need an S³ Intentional Interim Pastor if your numbers have plateaued or declined over the past five to seven years. You must engage in strategic planning to stop the attrition and revitalize your church before you call your next pastor.

5. Your church may need an S³ Intentional Interim Pastor if over the past ten years the average age of the persons attending your church has increased by five or more years, and you are having difficulty attracting younger families with children. You are ready to consider transitions and changes before you call your next pastor.

6. Your church may need an S³ Intentional Interim Pastor

if your former pastor served your church for more than ten years, during which time you have fallen into stale patterns that lack continual innovation. You must sharpen the life and ministry of your church before you call your next pastor.

7. Your church may need an S³ Intentional Interim Pastor if you know you are facing a great new opportunity for ministry in the context where you serve due to residential growth and commercial development. You must proactively plan how you will respond to this opportunity before you call your next pastor.

8. Your church may need an S³ Intentional Interim Pastor if your church is at a hinge point in its life and ministry. You must consider choices such as relocation, merger, or adoption by or of another church, before you call your next pastor.

9. Your church may need an S³ Intentional Interim Pastor if you believe you must reconsider your denominational affiliation. Your church is diverging from your denomination and you must clarify your denominational allegiance before you call your next pastor.

10. Your church may need an S³ Intentional Interim Pastor if there are other opportunities and challenges not mentioned in this list that you must prayerfully and strategically consider before you call your next pastor.

Consider the Benefits of Calling a *Seasoned*, *Skilled*, and *Strategic* Intentional Interim Pastor

Calling an S³ interim meets the immediate need for a pastor, preacher, and leader to ensure your church continues to be effective. Hiring an interim will also inspire confidence during a time of uncertainty.

Church attendance, giving, and visitor retention tends to remain higher when an S³ interim is serving the church. He brings continuity to the ministry, which helps maintain positive growth. Most committed members as well as casual or nominal members will remain in the congregation.

The S³ Interim acts as a buffer between past and future by giving the congregation time to release the emotional, relational, and spiritual connection to the former pastor. An S³ Interim presence creates space and time for the church to consider who they are and what they need before they call their next pastor.

An on-site S³ Interim provides oversight, accountability, mentoring, and training for the staff. Rather than burning out, the church leaders and staff team will remain energized.

Many churches do not know how to cast a vision. All churches would profit from using the time between pastors to discover God's Empowering Vision and to start living into it. Such intentionality instills an expectation that the best is yet to come. It communicates to your people and community that you are active, not passive. If you do not know where you are going, any road will get you there. But *every* church in transition, and traveling toward a destination, needs a

---

*Every church in transition, and traveling toward
a destination, needs a roadmap.*

---

roadmap. Without a vision, people either feel apathetic or pushed. With a God-given vision, the congregation is pulled, by God, into its future.

An S³ Interim will be among you but not of you. We mean by this that he can offer an objective viewpoint on problems beyond any congregation's nearsighted view. He can investigate and mediate interpersonal conflicts. He can speak the truth in love, rather than waiting for issues and problems to fester and become potential landmines to disrupt the next pastor's tenure.

Perhaps your church does not remember when they last had to find a new pastor. There is no one in leadership with the first clue of how to start. Your S³ Interim can guide your church in its pastoral search and increase the likelihood that you will call a pastor who fits your culture, values, vision, and programs.

Strengthening your church during the interim season sets up the next pastor for tremendous success. The church leaders, with the S³ Interim's help, take down roadblocks. Everyone starts to sing the same song, and in harmony. A shared vision unites the church as the church looks toward its promising future. They believe the best days are before them, and a P³ Lead Pastor will come to a church on an upward trajectory—ascending and actively living into their God-given future.

A good S³ interim identifies and nurtures new people to rise up to be trained and serve. The transitional period is a hothouse for germinating, nurturing, growing and motivating people into a leadership mindset.

Soaring with a Sully

Churches in pastoral transition need the Sully Sullenberger's of the evangelical pastoral world—the gray-haired guys with combat experience who have been flying the planes for a long time. When the former pastor leaves, churches need a Sully who does not get rattled or flustered when something goes wrong, like an associate pastor flaming out. These experienced ministry pilots know what to do if the engines fail and how to land the plane so that everyone can walk away safely. When I (Tom) board a flight, I take extraordinary comfort in seeing an older gray-haired pilot in the left-hand seat doing the pre-flight checklist.

At some point your church will be between pastors. This opportune moment (see Ephesians 5:5-6) is a tipping point that can move your church into more excellent health, vitality, and fruitfulness. Don't waste what can be the most significant time in your church's history. Use today to prepare your church, Jesus' Church for what He wants to do tomorrow. Don't drift through a pastoral transition; instead, soar upwards during this opportune moment.

You need a top gun. You need a Sully—an S³ Intentional Interim Pastor who will almost guarantee that your next P³ Lead Pastor will be of the same caliber and quality.

CALL TO ACTION

- Determine if your church needs and desires an S³ Intentional Interim Pastor.

- Seek third-party guidance to discover, discern, and call the best possible S³ Intentional Interim Pastor.

- Place great confidence in your S³ Intentional Interim Pastor to guide your church effectively so you can soar between pastors.

CALL TO PRAYER

- Pray for God's guidance to lead you to the best possible S³ Intentional Interim Pastor for your church.

- Pray that your church will follow the seasoned, skilled, and strategic guidance of your S³ Intentional Interim Pastor.

- Pray without ceasing for your next pastor, hopefully a P³ Lead Pastor.

"IPM Saved This Church."

Jane Roberts,
Reporter with the Daily Memphian, *www.dailymemphian.com*

G race Church had lost thousands of members. With the quick departure of two lead pastors, the church became known as a graveyard for pastors.

The church's most significant challenge was lost confidence and trust in their leaders who often served uninterrupted for decades. Prior to the arrival of their interim pastor, several congregational meetings were pleas for the elders to step down. Yet, they were self-appointed and nothing changed except frustration deepened and anger grew.

Facing yet another stretch between pastors, the church called on Interim Pastor Ministries for help. It was a call with eternal consequences as the church called a seasoned, skilled, and strategic IPM Intentional Interim Pastor.

For 30 months, their IPM Interim Pastor sorted through layers of congregational mistrust and hurt as he conducted mediation and intervention. He conducted 300 listening interviews with congregants, formed and lead a transition team of 20, helped rewrite its constitution, conducted leadership training, guided the Pastoral search committee, and lead the church in discovering a clear vision of what it wanted to be and do.

Trying to create an opportunity for younger men to have a voice on the board of elders, their IPM Interim Pastor asked five of the most senior members to take "emeritus" status. They would be honored as church leaders but would no longer have a vote on the board. The move caused anger and hurt. Four of the five left, and another 25 family and friends followed.

"My goal is to work with the existing leadership," their interim pastor said. "The number one preference is that all the existing leadership will stay and buy into the change and be part of the process. That is the healthiest way. But some are not going to be able to make that transition." "You can't come in and dominate or assert power," their interim said. "You have to build trust and credibility. You have to help the church come to its own decisions. I lead a process so they can make their own decisions."

"I had no expectation other than the fact we needed to let him do all the things he did," said the chairman of Grace Church board of elders. "He did what was necessary to help us."

Grace Church's Executive Pastor said the church owes IPM and the Interim Pastor they supplied a *massive debt* for what they accomplished. He summed up this organization's contribution when he said, "IPM saved this church."

Our Passion

We have written this book because we have a passion and a calling to help churches soar between pastors. Tom comes to this book from the perspective of a life of ministry with churches between pastors, and almost a decade as President of Interim Pastor Ministries (IPM) at InterimPastors.com.

George comes to this book from almost 50 years as a church planter, revitalization pastor, researcher, consultant, coach, denominational executive where one of his foci has been to work with or guide processes for churches between pastors.

The material in this book is not intended to sell the services of either Interim Pastor Ministries or the mentoring of George Bullard. It is simply to offer insights into how churches can soar between pastors as they journey toward reaching their full Kingdom potential.

There are many systems, various denominations, and hosts of parachurch organizations throughout North America who address interim ministry. IPM is just one of them. We encourage you to consider the principles and practices in this book regardless of where you connect for an interim pastor when you need one.

At the same time, we would be remiss if we did not at least introduce you to the services of IPM, so this can be one of the choices you consider. IPM has 200 pastors who are members of IPM and either preparing for or currently serving as an S³ Intentional Interim Pastor.

About IPM

IPM is the largest evangelical Protestant organization dedicated to providing S³ Intentional Interim Pastors. Since 1990, IPM has served more than 1,300 churches. IPM services 80 or more churches at any given time.

Each IPM S³ Intentional Interim Pastor embodies a unique spiritual call of God to serve churches during the transitional period. They see their temporary yet intimate relationship with churches as a calling and not just a job. They desire to connect the church with a renewed sense of God's empowering mission and vision for the church.

All IPM pastors are at least 50 years old, have a 15–35-year track record of effective ministry, and are *skilled*, *seasoned*, and *strategic*. They are thoroughly trained and vetted for IPM membership. They receive continuing education and have at their disposal a multi-layer resource we call the *IPM Institute*. Their experience, training, knowledge, and coaching builds them into specialists in interim ministry.

Every year, we invite our members to Trinity International University, near Chicago, for our annual *Summit Conference*. We have three days of in-depth interim training. We marvel at the godly, high-impact S³ Intentional Interim Pastors God directs to us. Many have some good grey hair, for God has seasoned them for this encore career.

When they serve as an S³ Intentional Interim Pastor, they

are bolstered by an additional vital resource—one of IPM's 30 trained coaches. We put our reputation on the line every time we send an interim pastor out, so we are rigorous gatekeepers.

While IPM pastors do not have a checkbox, cookie-cutter system into which we press every church we serve, we do have an intentional process that provides an immediate sense of relief that someone is on board who knows what he is doing, and things are going to be all right in the long-run.

The IPM pastor does not act unilaterally. They will build and work with a transition team of church leaders, associate pastors, and other faithful, mature, resourceful church members. Rest assured their ministry is about your church being significant in God's Kingdom.

The model IPM uses is seen in many key New Testament churches leaders—notably Timothy and Titus. Paul's letters to these two are specifically about church restoration and renewal by interim pastor leaders. As with these biblical characters, IPM's S³ Intentional Interim Pastors cannot stay and be your next pastor. IPM, the S³ Intentional Interim Pastor, and the client church will all agree with this prohibition in writing. Therefore, the S³ Intentional Interim Pastor is there to give everything he has to your church and is not posturing the be your P³ Lead Pastor.

You can also rest assured an S³ Intentional Interim Pastor will serve your church well. He can help you to take the actions presented in this book. With this guidance and wisdom, your church can have a strong pastoral transition, become healthier, and move forward with clear direction. This preparation will lead you through a field of higher-caliber candidates and to a pastor that is a much better fit for longevity in your Church.

Contact Interim Pastor Ministries at:

Interim Pastor Ministries
PO. Box 113
Orleans, MI 48865
800.501.7117
info@interimpastors.com
www.interimpastors.com

Contact IPM and we will be glad to arrange to share with your church our five-stage intentional process to help your church soar between pastors. Even more, we will begin praying for your specific church and its future.

About the Authors

TOM HARRIS

Tom is a nationally recognized leader in the growing field of intentional interim ministry. For more than 16 years, Tom served ten churches as an Intentional Interim Pastor in Virginia, North Carolina, Arizona, California, Nebraska, Georgia, and Michigan.

Since 2012, Tom has served as the President of Interim Pastor Ministries (IPM), an organization begun in 1990 to serve and strengthen churches during pastoral transition for greater effectiveness. Through its team of 180 seasoned, skilled and strategic interim pastors, IPM currently serves 80-100 churches at any one time, and since 1990, cumulatively, it has served over 1300 churches.

Tom's passion is the beauty, vitality, and effectiveness of Jesus' bride, the Church. This book distills his decades of experience as a Pastor, Intentional Interim Pastor, and President of Interim Pastor Ministries.

Tom is a graduate of Washington Bible College and Dallas Theological Seminary. In 2017, Capital Seminary and Graduate School of Lancaster Bible College recognized Tom's lifetime achievements awarding him a Doctor of Divinity degree.

Connect with him at *tom@interimpastors.com*

George Bullard

George serves as a Strategic Thinking Mentor following more than 50 years of congregational and denominational ministry. He has served congregations as a church planter, a church revitalization pastor, and an interim pastor. He has served denominations in local, regional, national, and global positions.

He began serving as a consultant and coach to congregations, denominations, and parachurch organizations in the 1970s. He has increased his expertise and insight as he moved through various roles with congregations and denominations from more than 50 denominations in North America. He has provided advice, counsel, and training to Interim Pastor Ministries for several years.

George is the author of several books. Among them are the following:

- *Shaping a Future for the Church in Changing Communities* (co-author)
- *Pursuing the Full Kingdom Potential of Your Congregation*
- *Every Congregation Needs a Little Conflict*
- *FaithSoaring Churches*
- *Captured by Vision: 101 Insights to Empower Your Congregation*

He is transitioning into his next phase of ministry, the theme of which is Forthtelling Innovation, where he will serve in a mentoring role and publish a blog, articles, and books.

Connect with him at *BullardJournal.org* or *BullardJournal@ gmail.com.*

Made in the USA
Monee, IL
14 July 2021